HANDBOOK FOR
COMMUNITY PROFESSIONALS

Consultants

Frank Itzin
Jerrold Voss

Produced Under Grant No. AA-4-70-037-03-S1
United States Department of Health, Education, and Welfare
Administration on Aging

HANDBOOK FOR
COMMUNITY PROFESSIONALS
An Approach for Planning and Action

By

MERLIN A. TABER, Ph.D.

Professor, Jane Addams Graduate School of Social Work,
University of Illinois at Urbana-Champaign, Illinois

DONALD E. LATHROPE, Ph.D.

Director, Division of Social Work Education and
Division of Applied Behavioral Sciences,
George Williams College, Downers Grove, Illinois

SUZANNE C. SMALL, M.S.W.

Staff Associate, Action on Aging Project of Champaign
County, Illinois

NAOMI REMPE, M.S.W.

Staff Associate, Action on Aging Project of Champaign
County, Illinois

MARILYN FLYNN, M.S.W.

Instructor, Jane Addams Graduate School of Social Work,
University of Illinois at Urbana-Champaign, Illinois

JOHN J. COYLE, M.S.W.

Executive Director,
United Way of Champaign County, Illinois

CHARLES C THOMAS • PUBLISHER
Springfield • Illinois • U.S.A.

Published and Distributed Throughout the World by
CHARLES C THOMAS • PUBLISHER
BANNERSTONE HOUSE
301-327 East Lawrence Avenue, Springfield, Illinois, U.S.A.

© *1972 by* CHARLES C THOMAS • PUBLISHER
ISBN 0-398-02426-X
Library of Congress Catalog Number: 76-172466

To those people on "the cutting edge"—
who have accepted the challenge
of creating positive change.

PREFACE

This handbook is the result of a three-year project sponsored by the United Community Council of Champaign County, Illinois, in cooperation with the Jane Addams Graduate School of Social Work, University of Illinois, Champaign-Urbana campus. The project, formally known as "Planned Change in Social Provisions for the Aged," was funded by the United States Department of Health, Education, and Welfare, Administration on Aging, Grant Number AA-4-70-037-03-S1, and by the United Community Council. This financial support is gratefully acknowledged.

Co-Principal Investigators for the project were Dr. Merlin Taber, Jane Addams School of Social Work; and Dr. Donald Lathrope, Jane Addams School of Social Work and now Director of Social Work Education, George Williams College. Mr. John Coyle, Executive Director of the United Community Council served as Project Administrator. Mrs. Suzanne Small and Mrs. Naomi Rempe were the Staff Associates, and Mrs. Marilyn Flynn was the Research Associate. Project Consultants were Mr. Frank Itzin, Jane Addams School of Social Work; and Mr. Jerrold Voss, Urban Planning, University of Illinois and Harvard University.

The overall purpose of the project was to develop and then to implement a workable approach for directed change in community services for older people. The approach developed, which used recent ideas and research reports to achieve a new framework for action, was tried for one year in Champaign County by one full-time and one half-time social worker, Mrs. Rempe and Mrs. Small. They were the Community Professionals. Assistants were used to gather the information necessary for action. The trial effort was known locally as "Action on Aging." In addition to active participation in the development of the approach, all project members served as an advisory body for the one-year trial period and for the collection of data.

Based upon the many positive changes initiated or obtained during the trial period for this approach, this handbook was written as a practical guide on how to create community change. Mrs. Small and Mrs. Rempe were primarily responsible for writing the handbook. Appendix II was written by Mrs. Flynn.

Numerous groups and individuals have made contributions to the project and the handbook. The United Community Council's Committee on Aging recognized the need for concerted effort in order to bring about change in the area of aging and therefore sought the assistance of the Jane Addams Graduate School of Social Work. Members of the committee who gave special impetus to the project included Mr. Charles Dixon, Mrs. Helen Harland, Mr. Neil Smith, Dr. Harold Colvin, and Mrs. Fred Proff.

Graduate students at the Jane Addams Graduate School of Social Work, under the supervision of Dr. Taber and Mr. Ernest Gullerud, conducted research that led to the application for funds to the Department of Health, Education, and Welfare for the project. The students included Mrs. Lyn Plath, Mrs. Janice Rothbaum, Mrs. Julia Kling, Mrs. Dianne Wicker, Mrs. Elaine Smuczynski, Mr. Frederick Stein, Mr. Troy Simpson, Jr., Miss Dorothy Evans, and Mr. Verlyn Wenndt.

The project was enhanced greatly by the most able assistance of Mrs. Mary Brockett, who did a great deal of work in the collection of social provisions data. Other assistants included Mrs. Mary Meyer, Mrs. Margaret Campbell, Mr. E. Robert Williams, and Mrs. Teresa Williams.

The Board of Directors of the United Community Council are to be commended for their sponsorship of the project, for their financial support, and for the autonomy that they allowed the project in the trial effort.

The citizens of Champaign County, particularly those persons who were involved directly in the efforts by helping to bring about change, played a necessary and important role in the successful trial of the approach. Mrs. Janie Bloomer and Mrs. Mary Slack must be commended highly for valuable service to their community.

Several people made significant contributions to this handbook by providing constructive criticism and suggestions. Especially helpful were the comments by Dr. Samuel Weingarten, Dr. Ruth Heifetz, Mr. Charles Henderson, Mr. William Hockstad, Mrs. Judy Sherwood, and Mrs. Paula Dade.

The competent editorial assistance of Mrs. Lois Haig, and the faithful services of Mrs. Maxine Thomas, secretary, made it possible to share the approach with others.

CONTENTS

Very specific

(Good - Brief)

HANDBOOK FOR
COMMUNITY PROFESSIONALS

Chapter 1

INTRODUCTION

IN twentieth-century United States, the realization has dawned that society must be more rational about the major social institutions for health care, education, and social welfare that exist in every community. The "quality-of-life" concept, while still vague, does capture this concern with the notion that a modern society must provide something more for its people than consumer goods. This "something more" is obviously the availability and accessibility to the citizen of adequate education, recreation, health services, and counseling or back-up services for people who have special difficulties.

Choosing a neighborhood in which to live illustrates this concern with quality of life or adequacy of social institutions in the community. In choosing a neighborhood, one wants to know that he is safe, that he can travel conveniently to other places he chooses to go, that there will be cultural and recreational facilities available to him; that the schools, churches, social agencies, and health facilities are adequate and accessible. Finally, one is interested in something that can only be called "community spirit." Are the people in the neighborhood or this community concerned about their public responsibilities so that there is enough money and energy available to maintain a decent environment, to help those who are distressed, and to develop the social as well as the material life of the community?

Attempts to improve the quality of life cannot wait upon development of a science or a technology of community-service institutions. Despite lack of exact knowledge and adequate tools, increasing thousands of persons are employed in every community to organize, plan, and adjust these growing community services. The war on poverty, with its controversial and uncertain outcomes, is a dramatic example of a major effort to reorient and improve community services. The growing community mental-health movement of the past ten years is a parallel example.

These two movements seem to be based on the premise that too often the people who need community services the most receive the least. These movements are attempts to improve life through community intervention rather than an individual-treatment approach. More and more observers agree that attempts to adjust large numbers of people to existing community institutions have proven to be neither successful, efficient, intelligent, nor humane. There is now interest in adjusting community institutions to better meet the needs of the populace who need the services.

Confusion and controversy surround the war on poverty and other new movements. Nevertheless, they represent a serious and large-scale effort to rationalize the deployment of social resources to the population through the community-service institutions. Certainly it could be argued that such rationalization is not new—one could cite the prophets of social engineering; one could point to the charity organization movement of one hundred years ago; one could argue that visionary leaders in politics and social services have always concerned themselves with the systematic development and deployment of resources through community-service institutions. All this is true, but in the past ten years, society has begun to use tax monies on a large scale in order to employ a new breed of community professional whose concerns are bounded not by the individual person he is talking with, but by the overall community system of human service.

Several different approaches for the community professional have emerged. Three that are widely current today are the traditional community organizer, the social activist, and the advocate. Each of these approaches embodies a different set of goals and different behaviors for the community worker.

The traditional role of the community organizer is primarily one of facilitating an effective process by which those with whom he works (community leaders) can select their own goals and take action. He operates primarily through a formal structure and enables committees who purport to be broadly representative of the community to arrive at consensually accepted procedures and goals. Community problems and goals are apt to be defined very broadly in order to help achieve consensus. Generally, these goals or priorities deal with adapting, rationalizing, or producing new organizational structures. Details of allocating resources, employing personnel, and setting specific policy are usually left to the professionals who may seek committee approval after the fact.

In the role of social activist, the community professional is engaged in cause-oriented, more political activities geared toward solving specific problems in the community. The community professional or a small group of persons under his leadership selects and pursues a specific solution. This pursuit is single-minded and sometimes uncompromising. Resources for change are usually sought with the expectation that other causes will make an equal bid for these resources. The community professional's role as social activist requires that he be a strong and effective leader. The cause is stalemated if his leadership breaks down or if the zeal of his followers for the cause is lost.

In the role of advocate, the community professional is committed to a group of people, often a group of individuals who share some common needs and a group consciousness and who are on the receiving end of community services. The goal of the advocate is to produce a redistribution of benefits and a greater control over these benefits by the consumers or service users. In this role, the community professional places his skills, time, and knowledge at the disposal of the people. In the purest form of this approach, his actions are under the direction of the consumers.

In serving as an advocate or as a social activist, the strategies used in dealing with community structures are often those of confrontation and political pressure.

This handbook is not oriented primarily to any of the three approaches just described—working toward consensus through formal organization, social activism, or advocacy of consumers. Nor is it oriented to the broad and vague questions of defining community problems or setting community-wide priorities. Rather, this handbook is for the use of those community professionals who are charged to bring about specific planned change in the community-service institutions of the modern community.

The handbook offers a Bilateral Planning and Action Approach designed to assist the community professional(s) in reorganizing, reorienting, or developing community-service institutions to meet better the needs of a specific group of people. The approach contains the following:

- Terminology for its conceptualization and implementation.
- Ways of accumulating and translating information necessary for action, including ways of studying community change for planning purposes.
- Ways for the community professional to define and circumscribe his area of interest through the selection of target areas and the establishment of lines of activity for his work over a period of time.
- Methods and guidelines for effective action, which are flexible and focus on the strategic use of communication and negotiation in order to achieve definitive outcomes.
- Definition of a role that allows the community professional to operate flexibly as determined by the nature of a given situation, relationship to others involved, and the outcome desired in such a situation.
- Procedures for monitoring the community professional's activity and evaluating his progress toward short-term objectives through the use of an activity recording system.

Neither a new theory of planning nor a new ideological position is provided by this handbook. The authors have distilled the approach from professional experience and have drawn freely from social and psychological technologies in this development. The approach itself has had one trial effort in Champaign County, Illinois, with a population of 124,000. Appendix I presents an overview of the trial effort. Based on this effort, the approach appears to have direct relevance for a medium-sized community in which there is a functioning health and welfare network that is neither elaborately structured nor unwieldy in size. Aspects of the approach can be adapted to retain effectiveness for large urban areas or very small population areas. Although aging was the area in which this approach was developed and tried, the authors feel that it has a wider relevance and that there is merit in exploring the efficiency of this approach, with appropriate adaptation, for other social problem areas.

Certain guidelines and procedures detailed in the handbook may be helpful in a wide variety of situations where use of the total Bilateral Planning and Action Approach may not be feasible or possible.

The referents for this approach are a defined community of people who live near one another and for whom there must be organized an array of human services; and a community professional who is responsible for the following:

1. Improving the integration, efficiency, and effectiveness of this array of human services.
2. Dealing with various fund sources, auspices, and formal organization.
3. Achieving greater, quicker, or better service delivery in a given problem area with the end view of improving the quality of life.

The rationale, methods, or procedures for the selection of a specific community problem area are beyond the scope of this handbook. Type and interest of agency or organization employing a community professional, the availability of federal and local funds, and community interest are major determinants in this selection.

This handbook is offered to the new breed of community professional as an additional tool for his use. If a community worker's efforts are to have an impact on today's complex social ills, he must discipline himself to become more knowledgeable, more political, and more accountable than in the past.

The handbook first provides a background for the community professional by presenting an overview of the Bilateral Planning and Action Approach in Chapter 2. The remainder of the handbook speaks directly to the community professional by outlining the procedures necessary to implement the approach.

Chapter 2

THE COMMUNITY PROFESSIONAL AND
THE BILATERAL PLANNING AND
ACTION APPROACH

T HE Bilateral Planning and Action Approach is designed to
obtain desired change in selected target areas within a
specified arena of community life. This is done through the
strategic use of communication and the establishment of time-
limited negotiating alliances leading to the fulfillment of a change
plan.

The terminology employed in this description and throughout
the handbook is assembled in the Glossary. In order to facilitate
understanding, however, clarification of the following key terms
is essential:

Bilateral indicates that the community professional, on his own
initiative, approaches selected groups or individuals in an effort
to enter into reciprocal relationships around change ideas in
the chosen life arena.

Life arena is that sector of community life in which directed
change is attempted. This term embraces both the specific
group of people on behalf of whom changes are sought and the
institutions that influence the nature and quality of life for
these people. An illustration of an arena is aging persons and
such institutions as medical care, income distribution, and recreation.

Change ideas are specific ideas about changes in resource allocation, program, or policy. Neither feasibility of the ideas nor
the steps involved have necessarily been established.

Change aids are any existing or potential resource (e.g. people,
money, law) that may effect some change in an existing situa-

8

tion or in the condition of life for a specific group of people.

Change steps refer to the specific incremental, short-term, component actions that are necessary to achieve the realization of the change plan.

Change plan refers to the change idea(s) that has strong potential for being realized in a feasible, concrete outcome or goal. It is an idea for which some of the change aids have been identified, and some actual change steps have been defined and, at times, carried out.

Target areas for change are those concrete problem situations or particular areas for development (in a given life arena) around which the community professional focuses his efforts. For the aging, some illustrations would be nursing home facilities, retirement practices, and excessive taxation.

Line of activity is a coherent set of change ideas or change plans that the community professional is pursuing within a target area. Lines of activity are interrelated and potentially convergent, but for the sake of clarity in goals and efforts, each line is viewed separately.

The Bilateral Planning and Action Approach is made operational through the work of the community professional, who envisions desired changes and then acts to bring them about as follows:

- Employing communication and negotiations as the methods for inducing change.
- Maintaining a focus on desired outcomes.
- Retaining flexibility of plans and alliances.
- Using a work-planning system that involves feedback, evaluation, and correction.

The role that the community professional must assume when utilizing the Bilateral Planning and Action Approach necessarily dictates the following personal qualifications: (prof)

1. A demonstrated competence in defining, analyzing, and solving problems, i.e. an ability to weigh choices, to make decisions as rationally as possible, and then to be responsible for those decisions.

2. A personal conviction about the ability of individuals, groups, and communities to grow, to change, to help themselves, and to conduct their own affairs.

3. The ability and motivation to seek out and to assimilate new and relevant information, both about planning and the life arena chosen for change efforts.

4. Some skills in leadership, public relations, and especially community relations, i.e. the establishment of interpersonal relationships conducive to community education and actions.

5. An ability to establish good interpersonal relationships with others, e.g. other community workers, professional persons, lay persons, and persons in the life arena.

6. The personal characteristics that indicate an ability to modify goals, to have realistic expectations of self and others, and a willingness to share the spotlight of accomplishments with others.

For the required academic qualifications, a bachelor's degree is probably minimal, with a master's degree preferable. Academic training in the fields of social work, urban planning, community psychology, sociology, political science, adult education, or in an allied field (such as the action-oriented ministry) is desirable but not necessary. Recent research* substantiates that neither experience nor training are the crucial variables but rather that a critical factor is the personality variable or temperament. Some persons can work with people; some can work for people; some can do neither and end up alienating all concerned.

PLANNING

The community professional seeks constructive change on behalf of some group of people living in the community. This means that he must be knowledgeable about the people and the

---

*Poston, Richard W.: *Experiment in North Carolina,* A Report on the Community Services Demonstration Program of the North Carolina State Department of Public Welfare. Chapel Hill, North Carolina: School of Social Work, University of North Carolina, 1967.

particular community. Getting this essential information is the first planning step that is required in preparing to employ communications and negotiations strategically.

Information about the institutions that govern the quality of life for people in a given life arena is gathered both on a nonlocal and a local level. This includes social characteristics; social problems, issues, or unused opportunities for development; attempted solutions to the problems; and what the people in the life arena, the experts in the field, and the public, are saying, thinking, and doing about these factors. The social values operating in and around the life arena are additional important considerations.

The community professional also gathers information about local community change and studies the process, methods, and patterns by which change occurs. He is interested in learning how the health and welfare network changes; but he is equally interested in the change patterns of the overall community. Methods for gathering this information are discussed in Chapter 3.

The next planning step is to translate the information into feasible action, i.e. to generate change ideas, to devise potential change plans, to inventory and appraise change aids, to think through change steps, and to make the plans work. Translation of information into a plan of work requires successive narrowing of the community professional's focus. This involves the following steps:

1. *Selection of the overall direction for creating change.* This involves spelling out the broad "who, what, and how" of efforts for change, defining what is desirable, and indicating an avenue for moving in this direction.

2. *Summarization of those life arena problems and areas requiring development that are the most amenable to change.* An accompanying analysis, regarding who or what can bring about change and how this might best be accomplished, is needed.

3. *Selection of target areas for change.* These target areas become the focus of the community professional's efforts. Specific lines of activity emerge from them.

The sequential procedures for carrying out these steps are discussed later (Chap. 4).

Having established a program of work toward specific changes, the community professional then uses the methods of communications and negotiations to move toward change.

COMMUNICATIONS

Communications involve the exchange of information or messages between two or more people or groups by talk, writing, gestures, silences, and so forth. The community professional receives, sorts, and then relays information for the purpose of getting specific desired actions or reactions that lead to constructive change. The information is received and relayed through communication networks, i.e. lines of communication that already exist or are developed by the community professional.

Receiving information is part of the planning process. This begins as the community professional gathers information about the need for, and means of, obtaining change in a given life arena (Chap. 3).

Sorting the information, also an integral part of planning, begins as the community professional defines his overall focus and analyzes the information in order to select the target areas and to make plans for pursuing change ideas (Chap. 4). In making these plans, the community professional identifies potential groups that could take part in realizing change ideas.

The community professional relays information to those who have responsibility for taking action. These groups or individuals are selected because of their vested interest, key position, control of resources, state of readiness, responsiveness, or need for the information. In other words, the situation surrounding these people indicates that the relaying of certain information to them may provide strong impetus toward achieving some change viewed as desirable by the community professional.

The community professional advances change ideas through the careful dissemination of information and uses the individual communication networks he develops around lines of activity within each target area. Access to relevant information and ideas is a potent force that the community professional manages and uses.

The community professional provides pertinent information for the purpose of focusing previously undirected energy toward action or change. This may be concrete information about a source of financial or other assistance to a group already motivated toward change. He may provide a group or individual with the information necessary to eliminate an obstacle to change.

The community professional may short-circuit information in an effort to get a message to a selected place at a selected time. This includes speeding up information from national to local sources, forwarding information received directly to groups or individuals who could use or need the information to initiate change, bringing together groups or individuals whose shared information and action could bring about change, and working through the mass media.

EXAMPLE

The community professional gave a local social-action coalition group of the poor a copy of an analysis he had made of the health-service conditions in the community. Although written primarily from the point of view of older persons, it was applicable to other groups as well. Among other things, this paper included an analysis of problems in health and health-related services. This information provided the impetus for and was used by the coalition group to confront an agency that shared some responsibility for the problems which existed for the elderly, poor, and others.

The community professional attempts to communicate in a manner that is useful, timely, and at an appropriate level of specificity. Thus the style may range from a casual "Oh, by the way, did you know . . ." to a sharing of information that has been synthesized into a written recommendation for action. The style also may be direct or indirect, ranging from face-to-face conversation to a newspaper article.

EXAMPLE

In a letter and questionnaire sent to community employers about their employment and retirement practices regarding older workers, the community professional included a memorandum that presented the details of an upcoming new course on preretirement planning being offered by the local junior college. Although this course was listed along with many others on the back page of the local newspaper, this was not enough coverage. The memorandum directed the information where it was needed and was presented in a manner that called the employer's attention to the potential value of the course in his employment-retirement practices.

Several distinct phases occur in using communication. These phases are not necessarily sequential, may be duplicated or overlap in process, and are as follows:

- When efforts for change begin, the community professional sets the stage for contact by cultivating and preparing already existing lines of communication, such as the mass media and pertinent agencies or organizations, e.g. a coordinating council or planning-and-action groups that may be significant to the change pattern in the community.
- The community professional cultivates new sources of communication. He contacts and probes groups and individuals who might be potential change aids.
- As lines of activity are pursued, more pointed use of information and messages is made. The focus of the who, how, and what of communication is on realizing selected change steps.
- If the community professional makes effective and strategic use of communication, often others will begin to take the initiative in supplying and requesting information.

The community professional uses only the method of communication when developing negotiable situations or when negotiations are not feasible or advantageous. Most often, however, he employs the methods of communication and negotiation together.

NEGOTIATIONS

The community professional, equipped with a well-thought-out but flexible change idea that he hopes to negotiate into a change plan, identifies and approaches a group or individual whose cooperation he needs. If the response is positive, negotiations are begun to develop the idea into a change plan. The change plan specifies what each party is committed to contribute toward fulfillment of the change plan. Negotiations are completed as the commitments are carried out and as the plan is fulfilled.

The decision by the community professional to enter negotiations with a group is influenced and/or determined by the following kinds of information:

1. *The prevailing forces under which the group is operating and to which they might respond.* This may include the group's public or community charge, i.e. stated purposes for existence; the group's vested interest and the strength of its desire to satisfy its own functions and objectives; the factors, people, or pressures that motivated the group to positive action in the past; and the importance of public recognition, status, or an economic interest.

2. *The resources that can be allocated or reallocated.* This includes skills, time, money, physical facilities, community influence, energy, numbers of people, interest, and need.

3. *The capacity to negotiate a change plan and carry out change steps.* This capacity is based on determining the obstacles that exist and the resources that are needed by the group and can be provided or secured by the community professional.

EXAMPLE

A decision was made to negotiate with a particular grocery store for a home-delivery service after analysis of their vested interest, resources, and the probable obstacles. The manager had a vested economic interest in more business and displayed a concern regarding older persons' needs. Resources included available personnel, a good selection of groceries at competitive prices, and a solid reputation based on long-term adequate service to the community. In overcoming obstacles, the community professional anticipated the assistance that could be offered. This included access to a person who would make the deliveries and the names of older persons who were interested in such a service. During the negotiations, the community professional also offered to make and distribute informational brochures and to provide initial publicity.

In the negotiations, the community professional does the following:

- Suggests and explains the change idea and the desired outcome.

- Aligns the change idea with the group's vested interests that are compatible with the change desired.

- Shows potential use of the group's resources in relation to the desired outcome.

- Makes clear what he is prepared to offer the group in negotiating a change plan, i.e. ideas about that change plan, specific helpful skills and knowledge, professional work time, information about possible resources or change aids, and any short-term financial or physical resources that are available or advisable.

- Emphasizes that the major responsibility and community recognition for realization and continuation of a negotiated change plan rests with the group or individual.

EXAMPLE

The community professional entered negotiations with a public employment service to increase the number of job placements through a senior citizens' registry. His presentation emphasized the logical reasons for that agency's development of a registry and was based on recent, concrete information about older people's very low utilization of this agency, despite need. He stressed the vested interest of the agency in improving the employment services and pointed out that the change idea called for relatively minor reallocations of existing resources.

Initially, the chief obstacle that prevented the agency's concurrence in this change idea and its conversion to a change plan was the lack of manpower to publicize a new program and to carry out the job-finding and job-development aspects. When the community professional suggested the use of volunteers for these purposes, a different problem arose. The agency had a policy of confidentiality that prevented the release of identifying information to volunteers. The community professional helped resolve this problem by suggesting the use of coding procedures which ensured that the information would remain confidential. Acceptance of this procedure by the agency resulted in a negotiated change plan in which the community professional made a commitment to enlist volunteers and to draft the initial publicity.

When the commitments were fulfilled and the new program was

operational, the community professional discontinued regular contacts with both the agency and its new volunteer staff members.

The community professional also capitalizes on change ideas presented to him by others, including the people in the life arena. In evaluating whether a change idea is negotiable, he considers the following:

1. Does the change idea fit into the selected target area(s) for change?
2. What does the group or individual want from him in relation to his own ability to find or reallocate resources?
3. What is the ability of that particular group or individual to develop and carry out a feasible change plan?

EXAMPLE

A senior citizen called upon the community professional to express concern about the lack of variety in recreational programs for older people, especially for older men. He had several ideas as to what improvements could be made without major expense. He felt, however, that improvements would not be considered unless numerous persons and organizations presented a good case for them to the proper governing board. He asked the community professional to help him to motivate some community group who might be interested in actively pursuing this need. From prior knowledge about community groups, the community professional selected a group with good potential for pursuing this idea and proceeded to negotiate with the senior citizen about what each would do to interest and activate this group.

In negotiating a plan with any group or individual, the assistance the community professional offers varies with the requirements of the situation, but preferably it takes the form of limited, short-term commitments of help. He avoids plans and commitments that make him indispensable to the continued, long-term operation of the change after it has been established.

EXAMPLE

One change idea initiated by the community professional was to promote the formation of senior citizens' groups in small rural communities. After probing to identify interest, potential leadership, and sponsors, the negotiations that took place resulted in a meeting in each of four communities for interested churches, other organizations, and older persons. As featured speaker, the community professional attempted to motivate those attending to form a senior citizens' group and presented concrete suggestions as to how to get started. The talks and brief consultation were the only commitments negotiated by the community professional. Time allocated for follow-up allowed for only brief telephone calls. This minimal effort resulted in the formation of senior citizens' groups in three of the four communities.

Once a change plan is agreed upon, the community professional clearly identifies details of the plan and the mutual commitments of all parties to the negotiations. One way he accomplishes this is to send all parties follow-up memoranda about these mutual commitments.

Negotiations, including subsequent commitments of the community professional, occur only as necessary to carry out a change idea. Planned, regular contacts are time-limited and are discontinued when the commitments are fulfilled, when the other group becomes able to assume the responsibility for the change plan, and/or when the change is sufficiently stabilized to ensure its permanency.

When active involvement with a group stops, it is still important for the community professional to remain knowledgeable about the group as it relates to the change. Often this can be done without much effort, e.g. through newspaper articles or in general conversations. In other situations, he needs to maintain regular direct contact with the group. In order to ensure durability of the change, it may be necessary at some future point for the community professional to offer his assistance in the form of time-limited consultative activities or to respond to such a request by the group.

FOCUS ON OUTCOME

The Bilateral Planning and Action Approach is designed to help the community professional maintain an overall focus on intended, observable changes in the quantity and quality of community services. Achieving improvements may require changes in the financial support or the organization of community services. As a result, while work plans may call for focusing more immediate attention on structural or procedural changes in operating policy, staff assignment, or resource allocation, the ultimate focus is always on the direct benefit of the change to the people in the life arena.

EXAMPLE

In the target area of employment for the aging, a change plan to increase the number of older workers placed in jobs was negotiated with an employment service. This plan called for the establishment of an employment registry accompanied by a job-development component. The change plan called for some changes in policies and practices on the part of the employment service. Throughout the effort, however, the community professional maintained the ultimate focus on increasing the number of older persons regularly placed in suitable employment.

The achievement of overall and immediate changes requires flexibility in ideas and plans. Change plans can and should be reassessed and adjusted when new information reveals that a plan or some aspect of it is no longer feasible or desirable, or when a preferable, opportunistic situation arises. Large discrepancies between anticipated outcomes and outcomes actually achieved raise substantial questions about continuation. Reassessment could lead to negotiation of a revised change plan, abandonment of the entire plan, negotiations with another party, or use of communication as a single method.

The community professional retains flexibility in making decisions about entering into and withdrawing from any given situation. This flexibility ensures his freedom to act independently, often a problem for community workers affiliated with formal organizations who require consensus before any action can take place.

The community professional's flexibility is possible for the following reasons:

1. He initiates change plans that involve commitments that occur through bargaining, a give-and-take process. Commitments are mutual; and if not carried out by one party, the other party is released from his commitments.

2. He continually evaluates whether entering a situation or

being in a particular situation would lead to or had led to a "point of no return." Crossing over this point is done carefully and consciously.

3. He does not become an integral and indispensable part of any formal organization or structure. ? ? ?
4. He has relative freedom to operate, delegated to him by the sponsoring body.

EXAMPLE

The community professional negotiated with the owner of the local bus company toward obtaining improved service and reduced bus fares for senior citizens. Initially, the owner entered into a change plan and agreed to request a city subsidy to finance both the reduced fares and some major operational improvements that were necessary if the aged were to benefit.

However, when the owner subsequently applied for a subsidy designed only to maintain the existing level of service, the community professional withdrew his commitment to help to amass community support for a positive vote by the City Council. Instead, he communicated these same change ideas to officials of the city government who had, and subsequently used, the power to bargain the purposes and terms of the subsidy with the owner of the bus company.

In addition to flexibility, being effective in bringing about change through use of the Bilateral Planning and Action Approach requires keeping track of and on top of a number of things, assessing and evaluating numerous events, and making many decisions. The community professional must do the following:

- *Focus on results.* The community professional must keep to the forefront what he has done, where he is, and where he is headed in order to assess whether the change steps are being fulfilled and the change plan is being realized.
- *Safeguard time.* The community professional must keep track of time investments in order to relate and then to compare the time investments to actual outcomes in terms of the predicted outcome.
- *Have readily available and use important information.* The community professional must keep track of all incoming

and outgoing information and messages in order to strategically use and control communications, and he must keep track of the terms of the negotiations made in formal and informal bargaining sessions in order to negotiate effectively.

- *Receive feedback from actions in order to assess actions and plans.* The community professional must identify the results of his actions in order to make adjustments and corrections in his plans and actions.

- *Make rational and feasible decisions.* The community professional must consider such things as time investments and desired outcome, alternate change ideas and courses of action, and the consequences of selecting a given alternative in order to make decisions effectively.

- *Be accountable.* The community professional must record his activity in order to expediate his continuing accountability to the sponsoring body and others, as appropriate.

Focus on outcome and planned use of time is only possible through an appropriate record-keeping system. The complexity and changing nature of community work make focus on outcome and accountability impossible without self-surveillance. This handbook recommends a system that includes feedback, evaluation, correction, and a way to file information for easy access. Use of this system permits relative autonomy in planning and action. The details of this system are found in Chapter 6.

SPONSORSHIP, ACCOUNTABILITY, AUTONOMY

The community professional operates with the sanction and under the sponsorship of some established community group by which he is employed. The sponsoring group pays the community professional and provides the sanction necessary for his effectiveness. Ordinarily it is the group to whom the community professional is accountable and may be either a public, or private, community-planning body or council, or may be a community organization with a service function. For example, a state mental-health agency might use a community professional to develop local day-care services for the elderly who had been previously under institutional care.

In certain instances, the community professional may be paid by one body, yet he may be sanctioned and accountable to another body. For example, public or private funds designated for exploring experimental and innovative ways of operating in the community might allow the community professional to be accountable to a lay or indigenous group of concerned citizens in the life arena on whose behalf he is working. Ultimate accountability for reporting the results of such a project would, however, be to the public agency.

Funding and sponsorship also may come from national, state, or regional public or private sources. The community professional could operate locally under the sponsorship of a compatible volunteer board or operate without any local sponsorship. This might occur in communities with no existing or viable planning organization.

Although many different adaptations in structural arrangements can be hypothesized, additional experience with the Bilateral Planning and Action Approach is needed before a more concise definition of the structural constraints is possible. The greatest potential may exist in the following situations:

1. Community action and planning programs, particularly those with limited budget and manpower resources, e.g. community councils, health and welfare councils.

2. Governmental and private programs or projects charged with developing local services and with time-limited funding, e.g. Office of Economic Opportunity, model city programs, state child-welfare services, the Urban League, American Cancer Society, human-rights worker programs.

The relationship between the community professional and his sponsoring body concerning the constraints and autonomy that exist at various levels of decision-making needs to be defined clearly. Operationally, the Bilateral Planning and Action Approach calls for decisions to be made at several levels. At one level are the hour-to-hour and daily decisions that the community professional must have the autonomy to make, such as the freedom to select his own methods and tactics, to select negotiating parties, to make commitments by entering into negotiated change plans, and to make decisions about day-to-day operations. This freedom presupposes that on another level of decision-making, broad agreement is reached through active participation of both the sponsoring body and the community professional. This level concerns a definition of the life arena in which to attempt positive change, the direction of the overall efforts for change, and the target areas for action.

Between these two levels, there are others that involve such intermediate decisions as what lines of activity to be pursued or dropped, short-term outcomes to be sought, ideas or plans to be adapted or modified, steps to be taken, and time to be allocated. At these intermediate levels, agreement regarding the constraints and autonomy of the community professional must be worked out on an individual basis. The training, experience, and ability of the community professional, as well as the structure and available time of the sponsoring body, will be important factors in determining how many of these intermediate-level decisions will be shared with the sponsoring body. Constraints that are imposed here by the sponsoring body must be flexible and should be accorded frequent review so that appropriate changes in the working relationships with the sponsoring body can be made. For example, as the new community professional increases his decision-making skill, most of the constraints imposed at the intermediate level should be gradually removed.

Persons representing the sponsoring body must understand and accept the approach. These persons play a major part by advising and working with the community professional in the process of making the broad decisions that will culminate in the selection of target areas for change. At this point, however, it is imperative that they demonstrate active support for the overall approach and, even more specifically, for the premise that once target areas are selected, the community professional has relative freedom and autonomy in the daily operations and decision-making that are necessary to achieve maximum effectiveness. If these persons feel they must monitor or approve all decisions made by the community professional, then the Bilateral Planning and Action Approach will lose its effectiveness and might cease to be substantially different from the traditional, community-organizer approach that was mentioned earlier. One reason for the design of the Bilateral Planning and Action Approach is to avoid the time-consuming and often frustrating activity of seeking consensus among a number of people before an action can be taken.

Accountability to the sponsoring body is built into the approach through the use of a specially designed and innovative record-keeping system for feedback and correction. This system keeps the sponsoring body or group more fully apprised of the community professional's activities than is possible in most planning and action enterprises. This is important because the effectiveness and positive results of such accountability bear a direct relation to the level of autonomy that can be attained.

The consumer of services is beginning to play as important a role in the community as the more traditional service developers and providers. The need for community workers to be accountable to, and to involve indigenous groups in, the solution of their own problems is recognized. Unfortunately, what happens structurally in many instances of advocate planning is the same thing that creates problems for the more traditional community organizer; namely, the path to consensus among a group of indigenous policy makers is fraught with frustrations and unproductive delays. The efficacy of the methods of involving the consumer of service that have been tried by community workers is still in some doubt.

In the Bilateral Planning and Action Approach, unlike advocate planning, there is no direct line of accountability to the client group or the consumer of services unless representatives of the given life arena also happen to be the sponsoring body. There is, however, an ethical accountability to the consumer of services that is an integral part of this approach. It is one of the primary reasons for the focus on ultimate outcomes, i.e., how many more people in the life arena are served and how much more are they helped, rather than the prevalent planning focus being on new organizational arrangements.

Some ways in which the community professional can effectively involve the people in the life arena are as follows:

1. Collect change ideas about how to meet needs of those in the life arena better.

2. Collect, when necessary or appropriate, statistical data from those in the life arena.
3. Involve those in the life arena by communicating and negotiating as appropriate.
4. Develop helpful communication links between people in the life arena and those who are supposed to serve them or those who have the potential to help ameliorate their problems, and work to make them permanent through new or ongoing organizational channels.
5. Educate toward and then organize people in the life arena to act on their own behalf when there is little group identity or cohesiveness.

In pursuing any of these avenues, the community professional is careful not to become co-opted indefinitely by the people in the life arena, but rather, when long-range involvement is indicated, he might assist them to locate an executive secretary or group-oriented community worker.

Chapter 3

INFORMATION NECESSARY FOR ACTION

AS the community professional, your charge is to get some community action going—action that will result in some predictable, positive change. To work effectively, you need to obtain certain kinds of information. Planned change involves finding out and defining what is out there. It is necessary to know what life is like in the life arena, at the national, state, regional, and local levels. It is also necessary to know how the local community functions, how it changes.

Getting the necessary information requires time—time for a period of fact-gathering, study, and analysis before actively pursuing change efforts. Obtaining the information and using it to make some basic decisions and to prepare for action require from three to six months. It is crucial that your employer agree to make this time available. Information may be gathered by other staff. In such a case, you need to provide direction.

As a first step, it is necessary to gain some overall insight into what is currently known about the life arena. This information comes primarily from a review of the literature and the research studies in the field (at the national, state, and regional levels) and enables you to gain an understanding of the following areas:

- *Problems and issues.* What problem situations exist in the life arena? What are the major issues?
- *Social facts.* What are the primary characteristics of the arena and the people in it—social, psychological, environmental, economic, demographic?
- *Proposed solutions.* What are the results (if any) of attempts to improve these conditions? Who has tried?
- *Voice of the people.* What do the people in the arena think,

say, and do about their own problems? Do they have a group identity and cohesiveness? Is there dissension in the ranks?

- *Voice of the experts.* What do the experts say about the arena and problems? What are the prevailing theories?
- *Public opinion.* What is the prevalent societal thinking (attitudes) about the life arena?
- *Underlying social values.* What values are demonstrated in prior attempts to improve problem situations?

This information includes hard facts, e.g. the percentage of elderly below the poverty line and the percentage of elderly institutionalized, and is retained in a manner that allows easy and continued accessibility.

When an overall picture of life in the selected life arena becomes visible, this knowledge is applied to life in the local arena and is made relevant for local planning. Learning about the local life arena may be done through informal means, more formal procedures, or a combination of both.

GATHERING INFORMATION—LOCAL LIFE ARENA

An informal approach for gathering information about the local life arena is presented below; however, any method of more formal data collection should cover some of the same areas. This informal approach is general and may be carried out as such, or may be the foundation for building several methods, both formal and informal.

An abbreviated version of a more formal method of data collection which fits well with the following informal approach is presented in Appendix II.

Problems and Issues

Look at the problems and issues found in the literature. Review and explore any indicators for these same problems (or others) at the local level.

EXAMPLE

The life arena chosen for attention centered around older persons and one of the problems frequently cited at the national or nonlocal level concerned lack of a nutritionally balanced diet necessary to maintain health and vitality. This pointed toward the necessity of obtaining certain local information. This included identifying (at least a sample) and then tactfully interviewing a group of older people about their eating patterns, income level, physical condition, past life style and eating patterns, need for and ability to prepare special diets, use of vitamin supplements, knowledge of the importance of nutrition in their lives, and ability to use this information in practice.

It was necessary to determine what services existed which could help alleviate the problem (i.e. hot meal from social groups or centers, federal food stamp or surplus commodity programs, meals-on-wheels programs, availability of special or dietetic foods, consumer and nutrition information and training programs, inexpensive restaurants serving tasty and nutritionally sound meals).

Other indicators of the local problem were the percentage of older people taking advantage of such services, their knowledge concerning these services, and the relationship between income patterns of the elderly compared to the local cost-of-living index.

Social Facts

Get facts that identify and describe people in the life arena, such as population count, urban-rural ratios, economic level, age breakdown, marital status. Sources for this information include local studies and census materials.

Proposed Solutions

Find out what locally based services exist that help to understand, to deal with, or to alleviate the various problem situations identified in the life arena. What kinds of services are offered? How many people in the arena are served? How does this number compare to the total number of people served? How available are these services to people in the life arena, e.g. costs to client, accessibility, public awareness of the service, staff available, eligibility requirements, and procedural considerations?

This type of information about services points up problems and needs and provides leads to alternative solutions, especially when coupled with information about the social characteristics and problems of the people in the life arena, both locally and non-locally.

EXAMPLE

Substantial fees or restrictive eligibility requirements for services pointed to prohibitive problems in the use of those services by older persons. Many lived on limited and fixed incomes or on incomes just above poverty levels.

Although local employment services estimated that less than one percent of people they served were over 50, they made up over 25 percent of the local population. This indicated a problem situation where change efforts were needed.

Widespread contacts with community services are necessary to obtain this information. The community social-services directory is a good place to start to identify existing services. Ask people initially contacted to identify other groups that serve the people in the life arena. Although many of the services contacted may be part of the social-service structure, contacts also should include other service areas, such as businesses, transportation, churches, and informal social organizations.

Because your initial orientation is that of a learner, people in the community services may respond to questions in a relatively open and cooperative manner. Generally, people like to talk about what they are doing and to share their expertise and opinions. An initial rapport for later action may be established in these contacts. Questions that you ask may serve as a good first step toward stimulating ideas and creating a climate for change.

In addition to direct questioning, observation is another means of getting information.

EXAMPLE

The community professional investigated living situations for older people in sheltered care facilities. He found out what the formalized policies were by interviewing the head administrator for the facility. Then he talked informally with those working in the facility who had the most direct contact with the older persons and observed how they treated the elderly. He talked to the older residents, and observed the climate and the expressions on the people's faces. He looked for possible discrepancies between formal policies and operating policies.

Voice of the People

What do the people in the life arena think, say, and do about their own problems? What sorts of situations create physical or emotional difficulties for them? How is it manifested? What do they think society in general and the community in particular is doing to help? Do they see any community group(s) or individuals as their advocates? Where do they turn? Do recourses for their grievances exist? If so, are they aware of such recourses? In what way and to what extent do they participate in the definition of their problems? Do the people exhibit a feeling of group identity or cohesiveness with other people in the arena, or do they separate themselves from others in the life arena when discussing their problems?

EXAMPLE

An older person needed many supportive services directed specifically toward "senior citizens," yet he refused to identify himself as such and thus did not benefit from these services. Because of the negative connotations that have evolved around such words, he saw "them" as having problems, not himself.

The existence of this kind of pattern among the majority of people in the life arena could indicate that as a group, people in the arena had little influence, clout, or say concerning what happened to them and how their problems were handled. This information would have direct relevance for later action.

Learning to know and understand the people in the life arena and to gather change ideas may start with attending meetings they attend; visiting their churches, their recreational groups, their gathering places; listening to radio and talk programs they enjoy; taking the trouble to understand, learn, and when comfortable, to use the vernacular of those in the life arena, if one exists.

Seek the help of people in the life arena to get information directly from those in that arena. People are more likely to communicate freely their concerns, problems, and ideas with someone who relates to and shares their general situation.

Voice of the Experts

What do local authorities on the life arena think about its

problems, conditions, and issues? How do they feel about their own attempts to solve the problems and to resolve the issues? What would they like to do that they are not doing? What do they plan to do? Do they have a good grasp of the realities of life for persons in the arena? Do their analyses and opinions reflect a particular bias? Is their knowledge of the life arena and the people in it broad or limited in scope?

Public Opinion

What's the prevalent community thinking (attitudes)? What do community leaders think about the people in the life arena and their problems? What is their opinion about how people in the arena fit into the life of the community? Generally, are these people valued community members? Are they valued per se or because, by valuing them, the community may gain something desirable or prevent something undesirable from occurring? What investment do they think the community would or should be willing to make on behalf of the people in the life arena?

Some of the questions that will yield this information can be incorporated into a review of how the community changes as appropriate to the situation.

GATHERING INFORMATION—
COMMUNITY CHANGE REVIEW

Since change occurs continually in all communities, your effectiveness is partially dependent upon understanding how your community normally changes.

The informal community review presented here is designed to help you find out a great deal about community change in a relatively short time, perhaps 15 to 20 interviews. There are people in every community who are well acquainted with and involved in the community. Through appropriate interviews, information is obtained that can be applied in creating change.

The value of studying your community before attempting to create change can best be illustrated by examples.

EXAMPLE

Community "A" was an industrial community focused on rebuilding itself from a period several years ago when its economic base of strip mining collapsed. An emphasis on economic development pervaded community life. Many of the changes, such as the development of an industrial park, were made possible through massive private fund drives and donations. Federal funding had been purposefully avoided. The United Way was strong and powerful, resulting in part from the solid base of industry. However, it operated as an end in itself. The agencies which it supported were very weak. Health and welfare had experienced few changes and received only nominal community support. The fairly successful Community Action Program operated almost totally outside the health and welfare network, surviving with help from outside the community. There was no planning structure in the welfare area. Changes occurred because a few businessmen decided they liked an idea, rather than through any study of need. Other changes occurred because of help or sanctions imposed from outside the community (compliance to state laws). A definite power structure existed, although new leadership had emerged slowly over the last several years. The new leadership was less adverse to receiving federal help. Leadership was exerted primarily through money.

Community "B" 's economic base was not industrial but rather dependent on the state government and numerous insurance companies and other white-collar services. The community was somewhat divided between state government and local community. Although the community was politically oriented due to a large and extensive patronage system, community leadership came primarily from the private business sector. Leadership existed on two levels—the money holders and the "doers." The doers, operating through organizations and utilizing the money-holder's money and any possible help from the state government, became actively involved in the process of change. Change was often initiated by one person with strong drive and desire. The doers picked up the idea and carried out the change. Most changes were preceded by studies carried out or paid for by the community within an organizational structure, such as a Downtown Council, Chamber of Commerce, the United Way, and the Health Council. The United Way was seen as a tool for raising money for agencies rather than as an end in itself. An active planning body existed. Agencies were relatively strong.

As the community professional, you would operate differently in these two communities.

In Community "A," you would avoid close identification with the health and welfare structure. In fact, you would work as much as possible outside of it. You would operate on the basis that money for any given change would have to come from outside the community or be for a purpose that the United Way and the leadership really backed. Leadership involvement outside the area of money would probably not be of any great help.

In Community "B," you would involve the doers for verbal support and possibly for more. You would consider involving a community group in a special study, perhaps of some special area of need, as a step toward getting them involved in a change. Or, you might selectively distribute the results of your own study of the local life arena.

This kind of information and analysis about the community places you in a better position to choose what changes to attempt, what avenues to take, and what outcomes to expect.

Whom to Interview

Begin the interviewing with someone who has been well acquainted with the community over a substantial period of time. It may be your employer, the mayor, the head of the local poverty program, the editor of the local paper, a minister, or a businessman.

The selection of additional persons to interview occurs through a snowball referral method. Ask the first person interviewed to recommend others, and in turn, ask these people for recommendations.

Specifically, ask for recommendations of people in the community who meet one or more of the following qualifications:

1. Have a great deal of knowledge about various aspects of the community, such as business, politics, education, health and welfare network, or the selected arena of community life.

2. Are considered leaders or decision-makers in the community, or some segment of the community.

3. Hold positions of leadership, such as a mayor or commissioner.

4. Hold positions that provide potential for community leadership in some form, such as the editor of a newspaper, director of a radio station, or a community leader indigenous to the life arena.

5. Have played a vital part in some of the significant community changes or failures.
6. Could provide information based on being part of, having knowledge about, or having involvement with, certain segments of the community, such as indigenous leaders of minority groups, e.g. by reason of race, economics, age, or nationality.

Depending upon the life arena, the request for recommendations of people to interview can be more or less specific than those mentioned above. In addition, not all persons you interview need to be recommended. For example, no one may suggest that you talk to the mayor, but you may choose to do so anyway. What is important is that you get a view of the community and community changes from a number of viewpoints.

Interviewing Style

Conduct the interviews flexibly, without the use of a highly structured and formal questionnaire. Prepare guiding questions and use them appropriately. However, prepared questions do not always elicit the kind of information desired. Explanations and examples may be required in order to get the kind of information desired. For example, information obtained should include how changes come about and how leadership works above and below the table. This requires some sensitive and intuitive probing.

Consider hiring some assistants to help with the community review. Information concerning certain segments of the community, such as the elderly or the poor, might best be tapped by having a person indigenous to that segment of the community conduct the interviews.

Types of Interviews

In early interviews, cover the areas presented in the following section. Later, direct interviews toward eliciting more detailed information. For example, after several people indicate that some person or group was primarily responsible for a certain change, interview that person or group representative for his views about the particular change. Question how he perceived the change, what motivated his actions, what he did to bring about the change, and whether he is satisfied with the end result.

What to Cover in Interviews

The special components discussed below are focal points for learning how a community functions and changes.

PROCESS AND PATTERNS OF CHANGE. One way to ascertain the process and pattern of change in, and to increase your comprehension of, life in a particular community is to center interview questions around significant changes. Include major changes that have taken place in the community over the last five years, change efforts that have failed, and significant changes that are underway or being planned. Change refers to the new and different about people, situations, or things, in addition to alterations in what exists. A list of areas to cover in questioning about change include the following:

1. What (in his opinion) were the significant changes?
2. Who (in his opinion) started the process, and how did he or the group(s) go about it? What spurred him to action? What other groups became involved? How and why?
3. How much money was involved and where did it come from?
4. What segment(s) of the community supported the change? How?
5. What segments opposed the change? Why were they in opposition? What methods did they use in opposing changes and how successful were those efforts? Have they been opposed to numerous other change attempts?
6. What was the community's attitudes toward the change (before and after)?

It is important to identify such things as dates, people, and money for each change, successful or unsuccessful, because they may reveal various trends, either of time or of certain groups or individuals who were involved in numerous changes.

EXAMPLE

In Community "C," an important organization deeply committed to community betterment appeared to be Women Voters Organization X. Estimates of the influence exerted by this group varied, but a rough guess would be that it was a significant catalyst for change. There had been no major reform in the community over the past ten years in which this organization had not been active. Political leaders derisively referred to this organization as "The League of Women Troublemakers" or "The Pink Ladies" and contended that they sought to take credit for change, when they had in fact done nothing. However, politicians admitted that the presence of accurately informed, articulate Organization X members at City Council meetings and other political affairs forced the political leadership to make itself more knowledgeable than might otherwise have been the case.

In examining opposition to attempted change, keep in mind that there are situations in which a given person, group, or segment of the community publicly supports and works for a given change, while privately and concurrently they oppose and obstruct such efforts. Situations are not uncommon in which apathy or passive opposition is the primary force that retards or defeats a given change attempt.

LEADERSHIP AND OPINION SHAPERS. It is important to find out who gets things done, who can change things, who is consulted about proposed changes, who has access to the money, who successfully opposes changes, who influences public opinion, and how all this occurs.

It is difficult to talk to people in the community about the power structure without a referent. Direct questions that are aimed only at identifying the names of those who comprise the power structure result in little knowledge about the dynamics of such a structure. One of the best ways to get this information is within the context of significant community change. The questions for which answers are sought include the following:

1. Is there a group of people or organizations who plays important roles in repeated change efforts? Is the leadership different in each change effort?

2. How diffuse is the leadership pattern? Does the leadership (whether or not it is relatively stable for different change efforts) represent a cross section of the community or just

certain groups, such as business, economic, professional, or political?

3. What role does the leadership play in change efforts? How do they operate?

Even if there are certain core groups important to community change, these groups may operate differently in varying situations. In many communities, there is no clearly identifiable or predictable leadership or power structure. This knowledge, in itself, is important for planning and action.

Remain aware of the existence of various styles of leadership and of making decisions. For example, someone may play a major role in change because he holds significant purse strings, but money may be his only involvement in any of the activities necessary to obtain a change. Other persons may operate through action, effort, and direct involvement. To further clarify some of these points, an analysis of community leadership patterns in City "H" is presented in the following example.

EXAMPLE

City "H"'s power structure and leadership formerly was only in the hands of wealthy, old family stock who had large local businesses. Leadership in City "H" was loosely knit and fell into several different types, i.e. the initators, the movers, the potential blockers, and those who influenced the voters. Diverse leadership patterns existed for the initiators of change ideas. However, change rarely occurred unless there was some individual or organization truly devoted to the cause or idea. With changes in higher education, it was a local lawyer; with the building of an auditorium, it was the state historian. Change within the city government was imperceptible, possibly because it lacked cause-oriented initiators.

The initiators approached the movers. The movers tended to come from the business sector and were concentrated most heavily in an area development association and the chamber of commerce. Their support was almost essential to change. The movers had four basic characteristics: (a) individually, they were active in many organizations and agencies in the community; (b) as movers, however, they operated primarily as members of organizations such as the above organizations, which both had strong, paid, full-time executives; (c) they had, or had access to, rather large amounts of money for both studies and implementation of change; and (d) they were not elected officials and were not dependent upon the political system. It was within this segment of leadership that most of the "new blood" existed, not only in the sense that many of these people were relatively new to this community but also in the sense that this particular leadership was almost nonexistent until recently.

The potential blockers were a somewhat diverse group. On a general community level, two identifiable types were found. One type consisted of the wealthy, old-family type mentioned earlier, who were generally not part of the movers. A second type consisted of the banking establishment. They were part of old-family types and/or movers. Other types of blockers depended upon the specific issues in question, e.g. the construction unions when it came to getting industry, one construction company and two large landowners when it came to property development, both city and county government when the issue required votes, and many ad hoc groups of the population when it came to a vested interest in specific voting issues.

Those who influenced the voters were generally considered the major public-opinion molders. This type of leadership was concentrated in city and county government. Those in city government generally functioned as legitimators of, rather than initiators of, change ideas. However, they had the authority to provide the structure through which change could take place. This structure most often took the form of a commission or committee where the "initiators" and the "movers" were brought together in a more formal organization.

Other factors regarding community leadership should be noted. For one thing, the locally owned industries had more influence and provided more leadership than did the large, nonlocally owned industries.

HEALTH, EDUCATION, AND WELFARE. As a community professional, you probably are concerned with some area of the health, education, and welfare network; therefore, you need to know how this network changes and how the network and its changes relate to other areas of community life.

EXAMPLE

In one community study, the community professional found that the change involved in building an addition to a hospital and expanding its services (considered significant by numerous informants) was stimulated by the business community in an effort to bring in more medical professionals, get a medical college, and become a regional medical center. These changes were sought to enhance their economic base by building upon service-oriented business rather than industry.

The health, education, and welfare network revolves around areas of health (doctors, hospitals, dentists, public health, visiting nurses), education (school, school boards, parent-teacher associations), and welfare (public aid, community action programs, economic opportunity councils, family services or counseling, United Way, mental health services, recreation, law).

In reviewing this network, the following questions are important:

1. What significant changes fall within the health, education, and welfare network? Are there other changes significant only to those in the network?
2. Were the changes stimulated by those inside or outside the network?
3. Who really makes decisions in the network—executive director, board of directors, citizen or consumer groups, local or nonlocal governmental bodies?
4. Does the network influence other areas, such as business, politics, religion, and vice versa? If so, how?
5. Does the community generally respond to proposed change in the network by support, opposition, or apathy?
6. Do agencies in the health, education, and welfare network, both public and private, have a reputation in the community for providing good services? Are they responsive to community needs? Do they cater to certain socioeconomic or racial groups? Are they viewed as innovators, or do they try to maintain the status quo?
7. Do agencies tend to be fragmented and highly competitive and to operate separately, or do they work well together with some semblance of coordination?
8. What is the role and status of governmental or government-sponsored services, such as community-action programs, parks and recreational services, public housing, and court services?
9. How active are the social-action and pressure groups? How

do they operate? Have they been successful in bringing about or preventing change?

One of the more important areas of the health and welfare network are the public, tax-supported services. Although many are controlled through state and federal governmental bodies, such as public aid, child welfare, or social security, they are administered locally and are influenced by the climate of the local community. Other public services are controlled more directly by local governmental bodies, such as boards of supervisors or commissioners, school boards, city or county hospitals, and public health departments.

In this area, attention should be given to the following questions:

1. What changes have taken place in this area? Have bond referendums been attempted? Were they successful or unsuccessful? How and why?

2. Have any of the changes included the application for or receipt of special nonlocal grants or programs to provide needed services, such as community action programs, public health grants, or special education services? If so, how were these changes brought about?

3. To what extent do the local administering bodies fulfill the charge given to them by their nonlocal controlling bodies? How much freedom do the local services have in making decisions about the provision of services?

4. How are the funds which are received, either through local taxation or provided to the local community, allocated? Are there funds received which are not allocated?

5. Do the public bodies cooperate with voluntary services or services of other governmental agencies? How is this cooperation or lack of it manifested?

One of the agencies in the health, education, and welfare network is the local voluntary fund-raising agency. Since the national organization is known as the United Way, it will be used to represent all comparable agencies. Through its campaign efforts, the United Way reaches into a broad cross-section of community life. Besides the primary medical services and the schools, utilized by many people in the community, the fund-raising campaign is another link between the general community and the welfare sector of that community. The United Way influences many voluntary service agencies and organizations in the community, either positively or negatively, because it holds certain purse strings.

EXAMPLE

In one community review, the community professional found a very powerful United Way that consistently went over its goal and had an extremely powerful community position because of its ability to raise funds. One of the reasons for this was the existence of large industries. However, the agencies that this United Way supported were, on the whole, very weak and powerless. The fund-raising drive was seen as an end in itself. There was no planning council which was associated with the United Way that might study needs and might evaluate current and potential services. The United Way exercised extensive control over the member agencies and over agencies or programs that might seek future financial support from them. A powerful Executive Director personally selected new board members mainly for their fund-raising ability.

A different situation was found in two other communities where the United Ways were less powerful and had difficulty reaching goals. In these communities, however, there was a stronger feeling that the drive was a vehicle for supporting the agencies, rather than an end in itself. The agencies were stronger and more effective. The community appeared to be concerned more about whether or not the member agencies were really meeting a need. Greater emphasis was placed on the needs of the agencies than on the ability of the United Way to go over its goal.

In a community review, include information about the role of the local fund-raising agency in the community and in the health, education, and welfare network. Consider the following questions:

1. What kind of agencies belong to the United Way?
2. What is the public image of the United Way and its member agencies? Does the community see the United Way and its drive as an end in itself? Or is it seen as a vehicle for getting money for the member agencies?
3. Has the goal been reached in the last several years? What kind of goal is set and how is it determined? Is it related to

amounts collected in previous years or oriented more toward agency needs? Do the agencies set their individual
goals based on client needs or on the community's ability
to reach monetary goals?

4. How are new agencies and organizations admitted?

5. What role do the member agencies play in the United Way
and its decision making? How does the United Way use
money to influence or control the member agencies?

6. How is the money that is raised allocated to the agencies?

HISTORICAL PERSPECTIVE OF THE COMMUNITY. Some knowledge
of the historical development of the community is necessary so
that community change can be seen in its proper perspective.
What past events, changes, or conditions have had a significant
impact on the development of the community? This may include
development in terms of type and strength of economic growth,
population growth; ethnic, cultural, or religious makeup; attitudes and values; community solidarity or division.

EXAMPLE

In one community studied, there was a heavy emphasis on economic development, particularly in the area of industrial development. This arose from the fact that the economic base of the community, strip mining, suffered severe setbacks thirty years ago due
to technological developments in other fields. Approximately nine-
tenths of the population had been employed in strip mining. The
economic base of the community virtually vanished. Rebuilding a
new industrial foundation became the overriding preoccupation. The
emphasis on this pervaded all segments of community life.

The Rural Community

Services offered on a county-wide basis often reach the rural
area in a nominal way only. Because this approach seems especially appropriate for smaller metropolitan areas and surround-
ings, it is important to consider the rural area.

The functioning of the rural community seldom is comparable
to that of the metropolitan area it surrounds. The dynamics of
change, leadership, conflict, health, education, welfare, attitudes,
and dominant values may all be very different.

A community review which covers the basic components just

outlined should also be carried out in carefully selected sample areas of the surrounding community. Doing a complete review of each small town in the county or other governmental units is neither feasible nor necessary. Selection of the sample rural communities depends upon the arena of community life chosen for change efforts, e.g. higher or lower proportion of youth, aging, or a higher or lower economic level. The number of interviews in the sample need not be as high as in the metropolitan area.

Since the most important activities in a rural community usually center around farming, church, school, and recreation, these are the areas from which to seek informants. In addition to a significant businessman in the area, e.g. banker, grocer, or publisher of the weekly paper, interview one or more persons from the primary governmental body in the county, such as a county supervisor. Home extension and women's clubs also can be sources of information.

Organization and Analysis of Information

After the interviews are at least partially complete, organize the information in written form.

The areas to be covered include the following:

- *Community history.* Social, political, economic and physical factors significant to the change process.

- *Change process and patterns.* Major community changes that have taken place in the past five years, changes underway or being planned, and changes in health, education, and welfare. Who, how, what, and when?
  Issues and problems in community change efforts, including reasons for success, reasons for failures or slowness of change, types of issues and change attempts that arouse conflict, and types of changes which are seen as significant.
  Common change strategies and patterns (both formal and informal), differences, and complexities in bringing about change.

- *Community leadership.* Whether leadership can be identified.

Whether leadership is diffuse or exists in a common core. How leadership is expressed.

- *Issues and problems in health and welfare.* Role of health and welfare in the community.

  Comparison of the changes and the way they took place in the general community with changes and the way they took place in health, education, and welfare network.

Steps in a Community Change Review

The guidelines that follow suggest steps for carrying out and subsequently using a community review. Improve or adapt these to meet the individual definition of needs in a given community.

1. Obtain general demographic information about the community.
2. Study and incorporate into a repertoire the areas to be covered and the general questions to be asked in interviewing.
3. Set up and conduct two or three interviews to obtain insights and leads for future interviews. Tape interviews, if possible.
4. Conduct remainder of interviews. Tape interviews, if possible. Contact additional informants for specialized knowledge, as necessary.
5. Verify, as necessary, important or conflicting information through further contacts or available written documents, such as newspapers.
6. Organize thoughts and materials and analyze tapes.
7. Write a draft of the community review.
8. Use the community review as an ongoing planning tool. Reread occasionally to keep information fresh in your mind and to make changes based on experience.
9. Use the community review per se, as appropriate, to generate action or to make decisions. Adaptations for selected audiences or widespread distribution are additional possibilities for use.

10. Use the community review as a long-term evaluative tool if a change effort is to be continued over time. The review also may assist in long-term assessment of additional community change efforts and, in this regard, may be helpful to many persons interested in the community.

Upon completion of the community review, you are now ready to translate all of the information obtained to date into a workable plan for community action.

Chapter 4

TRANSLATING INFORMATION INTO ACTION

WORKING STANCE

A DECISION must be made as to an overall direction for creating change. A working stance guides future decisions and action, spelling out the broad "who, what, and how" of the change efforts. It defines what is desirable and indicates an avenue for moving in this direction.

EXAMPLE

The working stance chosen by Action on Aging in Champaign County, Illinois, stated:

"Overall change efforts will be directed toward the provision of services which will allow older persons to remain as independent as possible for as long as possible. It will be directed toward providing older persons in Champaign County a range of choice in life styles, along an independence-dependence continuum."

This stance indicates that independence is desirable or should be part of the choice for life styles of older people. It also mentions that the avenue chosen for moving in this direction is through the provision of certain services.

How can you arrive at such a working stance? Obviously, the way in which a situation is defined influences the problems identified and solutions proposed. Although the community professional and the sponsoring body choose the working stance, the choice of direction is influenced greatly by the values and attitudes that are held by several different groups or individuals, i.e. society, local community, those dealing with the life arena both locally and nationally, those in the arena, the community professional, and other persons participating in making the choice. In order to determine these attitudes and values, you need to concern yourself with the following questions:

46

- What is the prevalent public opinion about people in the arena and their problems?
- What do the people in the arena see as desirable for themselves? How common or divergent are the attitudes held by people in the arena compared with those held by society?
- What does the community professional see as desirable for the people in the arena in terms of their overall life?
- In what way do the problems of people in the arena reflect the problems of society?
- What is the result of the way the local community deals with the given life arena? Are there choices open to people in the arena? Does it separate the life arena from the rest of the community? In what aspects of community life do the people in the life arena participate? Are these meaningful?
- What is the ultimate effect of the current national programs on the life of people in the arena?
- What is the direction of current thinking and research in the field in terms of what is desirable and what is undesirable?

Analysis of this information may suggest potential working stances that are in direct conflict with each other.

EXAMPLE

Some experts on aging support the disengagement theory—that it is a natural thing for older people to withdraw from active participation in society as part of the preparation for death. Much information and data can be found to substantiate this view. If this theory is accepted, then one viable working stance might be to work toward helping older people disengage themselves in a humane, expedient way from the mainstream of society.

However, other experts in the field actively disagree with this theory and believe that many of the basic problems of the elderly stem from the way a technocratic society has seen fit to deal with the aging, i.e. forcing them to disengage. If this theory is accepted, it leads toward a working stance emphasizing that older people should be helped to remain an integral part of all community life; however, because of the unfortunate, but now established, patterns of the aging, special corrective measures need to be taken. Considerable information and data also can be found to justify this position.

When such conflicts appear, as they might in almost all life arenas, then it is incumbent upon you and the sponsoring body to become as informed as possible about the theories and values that are involved. Then incorporate this knowledge and make thoughtful but arbitrary judgments.

After conflicts are resolved, there may remain two or more philosophically compatible potential working stances.

EXAMPLE

For the aging, such compatible possibilities might include the following:
1. Work toward the establishment or creation of meaningful roles for older persons.
2. Work toward group identity and cohesiveness of older persons.
3. Work to provide realistic opportunities for older persons to be as independent as possible for as long as possible.
4. Work toward helping the community change its attitudes toward older persons and to integrate them into all aspects of community life.

In selecting one among several potential working stances, consider each of them in terms of the following points:
1. The kinds of changes envisioned.
2. The ultimate effect of these changes on the problems in the life arena, on the people in the arena, and on the overall community.
3. The feasibility of avenues.

The choice of direction is made by you and your sponsoring body. You, however, take the leadership in determining and analyzing alternative directions that might be taken.

As information about the life arena, both locally and nonlocally, is collected, there are indications that certain problem situations are significant. Guided by the working stance, explore certain of these situations as they relate to potential change efforts.

ACTION WORKSHEETS

The Action Worksheets are a series of written summary accounts of information you have gathered about different problem areas or areas for development in the selected life arena. They also serve as a record of your analysis about what and who could bring about change and how this might be accomplished.

The Action Worksheets are active reference sources that serve the following ongoing purposes:

- They provide a means of considering alternative plans and actions and potential consequences of same for decisions that must be made, such as the selection of target areas for change.
- They provide a continuing source of ideas and information once action begins, especially for the adaptation of change ideas or plans.
- They serve as a potential resource when considering a new line of activity after community action is underway.

Appendix III presents an illustrative example of an Action Worksheet that was prepared during the Champaign County change effort on behalf of the elderly.

A suggested outline for consolidating information into Action Worksheets is presented here in annotated form. You can easily adapt this outline to reflect more accurately the parameters of your particular life arena and working stance. If your concern centers around areas for development rather than problem situations or conditions, adapt the outline as appropriate.

Problem Situation within the Life Arena

Make a brief statement of the problem situation to be dealt with in a given Action Worksheet, e.g. lack of low-income housing for older people.

Nature and Extent of the Problem Situation

Present evidence as to the nature and extent of the problem. "Nature" refers to the particulars of the problem situation—how it is manifested in daily life. "Extent" refers to both quantitative indications, e.g. numbers, and to qualitative considerations, e.g. severity of need.

NONLOCAL. Enter appropriate statistical information from the national and state level. Enter findings from relevant research studies. This information is particularly useful when local information is scarce or unavailable. Nonlocal data can lend support to or serve as a comparison for local data.

LOCAL. Enter appropriate information about local conditions. Information received from formal or informal research conducted by or for the community professional should be presented. It would also include available census information, research studies, need studies, public-opinion polls, and national and state information concerning the local community.

Existing Services Dealing with the Problem

Make descriptive statements about the services provided to deal with the particular problem situation. This would include exactly who is providing the service, any disparity between services actually provided and those which the organizations say they provide, and some notion about the number of persons served from the selected life arena in relation to the total number of persons served.

The kinds of services included here could be provided under public, private, or voluntary auspices; they could represent any segment of the community, such as business, or the health and welfare network; they could include regional, state, and national services available locally.

Much of this information is obtained in finding out about the life arena locally, as described in Chapter 3.

Change Aids

List the aids that appear to have potential for changing a given problem situation.

POTENTIAL SERVICE RESOURCES. List organizations with the potential to provide relevant new, expanded, or redirected services that affect the selected life arena. Include here resource ideas based on some tangible information, cues, and ideas that are unusual. These latter ideas will require further probes before real potential is ascertained.

One way of identifying potential resources is to ask who is providing what services in other communities. Are there services

being provided by national or state based organizations elsewhere but not locally? Are there organizations operating in other
communities which exist, or could exist, locally?

EXAMPLE

In the problem area of transportation for the elderly, a certain
volunteer organization operated a volunteer motor pool for the
elderly in many places but not locally. Locally, then, this group
was a potential service resource.

PROGRAM IDEAS. List new programs that operate in other communities around the country that could possibly affect change
locally. The description of such programs should be brief and
should give procedural information for locating a detailed description. It may simply consist of references for materials filed
in an easily accessible manner.

The greatest advantage of this section may well rest in later
formulating new programs relevant to the local selected arena,
suggested by synthesizing parts of several program ideas listed
here.

GROUPS. List local and nonlocal (regional, state, national)
groups or persons who could play some part in creating change.
List groups that are governmental bodies with some formal or
informal control over one of the existing services or potential
services, groups that have a vested interest in the problem situation, groups that might benfit from a change, and groups that
appear to be a causative factor in perpetuating the problem situation. Keep in mind that these are only suggestions, so remain
as open and imaginative as possible.

When listing these groups, mention ideas about how the group
or persons could help. Otherwise, good ideas will be forgotten!

LAWS. List any laws (at the local, regional, state, or national
level) that might be useful in affecting change in the problem
situation. This may include new laws about which the local community is still generally uninformed, laws that are not being enforced or uniformly enforced, or laws for which there have been
no test cases.

FUNDS. List potential funding sources which may help create

change. Local, state, and national governmental and private funding sources should be explored.

Possible Changes

List a number of possible changes that potentially are feasible for a given problem situation and may advance the working stance, keeping in mind your constraints of time and manpower. Base the list on careful consideration and analysis of the prior areas covered in the Action Worksheets, e.g. nature and extent of the problem, services being provided, potential services, and change aids.

Since this is a worksheet, be creative when listing the potential changes. Include a number of broad general ideas and more specific ideas. Ideas obviously will overlap and may range from the concrete to the very abstract.

Potential Lines of Activity: Alternative Options for Change

List potential lines of activity to be pursued in attempting to bring about the possible changes. Include any situation with the potential to develop into an opportunistic situation which lends itself to a potential line of activity.

SELECTING TARGET AREAS FOR CHANGE

Target areas for change are those concrete problem situations or specific areas for development in a given life arena around which the community professional focuses change efforts.

The selection of target areas requires informed, but still arbitrary, decision-making. Such decisions are guided by the working stance and are based upon the accumulation, organization, and synthesis of information, particularly the Action Worksheets.

Potential target areas are not necessarily synonymous with each problem situation as organized in the Action Worksheets. A potential target area may cut across almost all problem situations that are dealt with in the Action Worksheets. Conversely, another potential target area may be defined much more narrowly and may deal with only a small portion of any one of those areas.

The first guideline in the selection of target areas is defining the scope of the effort. This will be determined by the number of community professionals employed and by the length of time available.

The approach to target areas will be very different if the effort is for only one year instead of five years. You may have identified a problem situation calling for extensive change in a large bureaucratic structure or system. Because of the inherent difficulties in obtaining change in large bureaucratic structures, it is not feasible for you to attempt to create the large changes required in a one-year period. However, you may select this problem situation or some aspect of it as a target area and attempt to create one or two relatively discrete operational changes in the structure or to provide what might be an important impetus toward more substantial structural changes, with the hope that others inside or outside the structure might follow through after your withdrawal from the situation.

Given a five-year period, the selection of that target area is based on the consideration of more extensive changes and plans.

EXAMPLE

The community professional chose the target area of home health and help. This was done recognizing that although some services could be initiated or improved, these would only add to what already existed, namely, a series of small autonomous services that were ineffective because of the lack of coordinated delivery. Change was needed in the basic structure of delivery of health and help services. Given the one-year time span, the selection was based on the possibility of providing momentum for some first steps needed in bringing about these basic changes, namely, the establishment of a county-wide public health department and medical social services in the hospitals. The objective of the community professional was not to see these changes carried out, but rather to raise the interest level of those people in the community health sector who could accept this objective as part of their long-range charge.

The amount of effort suggested by a potential target area will necessarily influence the total number of target areas selected. One of the things to consider is the number of potential lines of activity that are foreseen within any target area. If, for example, only one or two possible lines of activity exist in one potential target area and six or seven in another, this will have to be taken into consideration in estimating how many target areas may be grouped into a manageable package for action.

In most situations, avoid the choice of just one target area unless you are confident that substantial, observable change will occur in this one area. Conversely, limit realistically the number of target areas selected so that your efforts will have a good chance of resulting in positive change.

The selection of target areas is made with the help of the following additional guidelines:

- *Need.* What is the greatest need in terms of lack of local services or programs to deal with the problem situation? What potential target area(s) does this kind of an analysis point to?
- *Adaptability.* Can there be an educated guess, based on past and current information, as to whether people in the selected life arena will adapt to change in a given target area? What about other persons necessary to the change process? How flexible or rigid do they appear to be? How does this compare with estimates of adaptability for other potential target areas?
- *Numbers and significance.* How many people in the arena will benefit from the change in a proposed target area and what will be the relative significance of such change in their lives? How much effort will be required? How does this compare to other target areas under consideration?
- *Time input.* Approximately how much of your time will be needed to bring about what changes in a potential target area? What changes are predictable using a maximum amount of staff time versus a medium or minium amount? How do such predictions compare to similar predictions in other potential target areas?
- *Flexibility of plans.* Assess the potential that exists in a given target area for the maneuverability necessary to take full advantage of opportunistic situations as they arise. Is there a wide variety of change ideas present for several potential lines of activity? Will this target area have great

change potential if certain situations arise? How does such an assessment compare to similar assessments for other potential target areas?

- *Viability of target area.* How viable are the possible alliances identified in a potential target area? Assess viability by looking at potential alliances, both in terms of the relative amount of usable vested interest which is present or forces operating and the number and severity of obstacles that indicate a capacity for negotiating.

- *Combining power.* Will change efforts in one target area affect desired change in other target areas that are being considered, and vice versa? If so, which ones?

- *Feasibility.* What are the given facts in the situation in terms of time, money, manpower, skills, and information, both for you and for the various change aids in the potential target area? When both sets of given facts are added up, how feasible does the choice of one particular target area seem when compared to others?

Since the selection of target areas involves a major decision directing the change effort, your sponsoring body should participate in the selection, either directly, or indirectly by designating or allowing you to seek the assistance of another group, or both. This other group could be an advisory one whose members are involved in various aspects of the life arena, or it could be a group of people in the life arena.

The participation of your sponsoring body and/or another group in the selection process includes active involvement in assessing or analyzing potential target areas or in reacting to your analysis of potential target areas and agreeing to those selected.

Take the following steps in the selection of target areas:

1. Assess potential target areas of change. This involves using the guidelines just listed to analyze the problem situations described in the Action Worksheets.

2. Attempt to group these potential target areas into sets of target areas that are interrelated rather closely. In order to do this, it may be necessary to synthesize further some target areas while dividing or eliminating others.

3. Analyze the various groupings, again using the guidelines for assessment whenever appropriate.
4. Select a set of target areas or one target area based on this assessment.

Once selected, these target areas determine the overall focus of planning and action. If, after you begin change efforts, the evaluative, record-keeping procedures reveal serious miscalculations in the number of target areas that you are able to handle, increase or cut down the areas, as appropriate.

SELECTING LINES OF ACTIVITY

A line of activity is a coherent set of change ideas or a plan that the community professional pursues within a target area. Lines of activity are not necessarily selected at the same time as, or immediately following, the target areas for change. Rather, they emerge as probes are made regarding various change ideas in a target area, as community groups respond to these probes, and as the potential for pursuing a given line of activity is weighed.

The selection of target areas necessarily involves some assessment of potential lines of activity within each target area and, at that time, you and the sponsoring body should reach agreement as to which lines are to be explored further. As you make probes in the community, some of these potential lines of activity may develop into tangible avenues for action. The selection of these specific lines of activity is then expedited by using an evaluative record-keeping system that provides feedback necessary to permit regular appraisal about the need to select new lines of activity or to drop those that are unproductive. Sometimes representatives of the sponsoring body may wish to share responsibility for selecting or dropping lines of activity. At other times, they may be used as a "sounding board" when making decisions. However, when opportunistic situations arise that call for immediate decision-making, you must have the autonomy to make these decisions independently. It is important that you reach agreement with your sponsoring body regarding the constraints and flexibility that will exist at this level of decision-making.

In making a decision about whether to pursue a given line, consider the same factors that are listed for the selection of target areas for change, such as need, adaptability, time, possible pay-offs in terms of meeting need, and feasibility. Once a line is selected, these kinds of considerations will continue to be important in making ongoing assessments as to whether a given line of activity is to be continued, to be dropped, or to be altered in some way.

Appendix IV presents an illustrative sample that details the development of one line of activity.

Chapter 5

GUIDELINES AND TACTICS FOR ACTION

T HE methods used by the community professional should facilitate the realization of desired outcomes. The central methods of action in this handbook, negotiating alliances and strategic use of the communication networks, were discussed in Chapter 2. This chapter presents more immediate techniques, tactics, and guidelines for employing these methods.

EXTERNAL GUIDELINES FOR ACTION

Negotiation and communication are made strategic in bringing about change through the consideration and use of the following guidelines.

Control of Bargaining Assets and Information

Bring to the negotiations those bargaining powers needed to motivate or assist the other group or party to make and fulfill commitments around the change idea and plan. These bargaining powers may include a carefully considered change idea; a rough estimate of the amount of time you can allocate; knowledge of the probable change steps and what is needed to fulfill these; knowledge of some of the prevailing forces under which the other group is operating; skills necessary to fulfill at least some of the change steps; information about need and about possible change aids; and short-term financial or physical resources. The physical resources might involve access to certain equipment, such as a mimeograph or copy machine. Prior to bargaining, evaluate and have in mind what bargaining powers might be brought to the negotiations by all parties.

In using communication, control the input of information. Before making a contact, evaluate the possible consequences of

58

mentioning other contacts, plans, problems, or of supplying certain information.

EXAMPLE

In bargaining with a particular grocery store for a home-delivery service, the community professional offered only those assets that the grocery store needed to reach and fulfill a negotiated change plan. These included knowledge of the procedures and problems of a grocery-delivery service that had failed, knowledge of this store's desire for more business without additional cost, information about a person who would make deliveries, skills and knowledge about the operating procedures for such a service, skills and equipment for drawing up an informational brochure to inform potential users of the service, a mailing list of older persons potentially interested in such a service, skills and information about other avenues for publicizing the service, time to devote to preparing the brochure and to distributing it initially and to drawing up other news releases. Among the assets or bargaining power brought by the grocery store were available personnel to take orders and package them, a good selection of groceries at competitive prices, and a solid reputation based on long-term adequate services to the community.

Recognition and Subsequent Use of Opportunistic Situations and Contacts

Evaluate all situations for the existence of a possible opportunity to realize desired payoffs. This evaluation will prepare you to act quickly, yet knowledgeably, if the opportunity does materialize.

EXAMPLE

The community professional was an active participant in helping to develop a telephone service that offered information, referral, and personal services for older persons. At a meeting with the staff of this service, the community professional presented his views on how to begin providing these services to smaller communities in outlying areas of the county. At this point, however, the plan lacked a concrete or viable starting point, since there was no suitable person in these rural areas with whom to begin working.

When a woman in one of the rural communities telephoned and expressed an interest in helping the elderly of her community, the community professional immediately set up a joint meeting with her and with the staff of the service. Having had prior acceptance by the staff regarding the plan, the community professional presented in more concrete terms how the service should operate in that particular community. The community professional followed up the meeting with a memorandum detailing the plan. The woman agreed to help develop the service in her community and to use the plan developed by the community professional and adopted by the staff of the service.

Timing

Anticipate the potential existence of a chance to realize some change ideas or plans and then plan so that you time your communication in a way that takes full advantage of any ensuing opportunity.

EXAMPLE

The community professional arranged a meeting with the local recreation department in order to present information and ideas about how they could adapt their services better to meet the needs of older people. With different timing, this could have resulted in nothing but just another meeting. However, the activity was strategic because the information was presented to the recreation department at a time when they were actively considering priorities and the allocation of money to improve their services.

Style of the Communication and Content of Information

Communicate the information in a style that is useful and at an appropriate level of specificity for the receiver.

EXAMPLE

If the community professional told a newly formed, rather isolated rural recreational group that "there are many available resources in this county for you to call for advice in getting started," this has little relevance. Instead, if he had said that "here is a list we've prepared of various resource people willing to come and help you to get started, and it tells you how to reach them and how they can help you," this information is obviously more useful.

Consider style of communication on two levels. The first level consists of various tactics, such as confrontation, consultation, seed planting or suggestion, or probings and questions. These will be discussed in detail later in this chapter.

The second level of communication style is concerned with

the medium used. The medium may be direct, such as personal contact, a telephone conversation, a presentation at a meeting, and a letter or memorandum.

EXAMPLE

The community professional synthesized information gathered about the health and help service needs of elderly persons, what services existed, and what services were needed. He recommended concrete, feasible first steps and directed these recommendations via a memorandum to organizations who could or should take responsibility for action.

At other times, the medium used may be indirect, e.g. confronting the Housing Authority indirectly through a series of letters to a newspaper editor and through telephone calls from persons in the selected arena that bombard the office. If one medium does not produce the desired results, experiment with another.

The Recipients of the Information

Try to reach those people who have the power either to negotiate or to act and who are receptive to the information and may persuade others in power to act positively.

EXAMPLE

In his efforts to obtain improved bus service for older people through a city subsidy, the community professional communicated by letter his ideas about desired changes in the structure and operation of the local bus company to the city councilmen, who were in the process of negotiating the purposes and terms of the subsidy with the owner of the company. When one councilman indicated receptivity by telephoning the community professional, subsequent information and assistance offered by the community professional were channeled through this councilman who had the potential to persuade other councilmen to act positively in the matter.

Dissemination of Information

Attempt to disseminate the information in a manner that keeps communication or potential negotiation alive and working. Get the information spelled out in the agenda prior to a meeting and in the minutes following a meeting. Get space in the papers

and arrange for radio and television coverage. Make follow-up
contacts once the message is delivered. Tell ten people the same
information. Rather than sending a communique just to the president of an organization, who may choose not to put the item on
the agenda, send it to all the board members, or particularly to
those with a definite interest and who may wish to bring it to
the attention of the group.

EXAMPLE

A health council, formed to work toward a county health department, was searching for something that they could be involved in
(before yet another referendum attempt) which could enhance their
overall purpose and retain the interest of members. The community
professional capitalized on this knowledge by accepting an invita-
tion to speak at one of their meetings where he presented relevant
information around some concrete recommendations that related to
one target area. He notified the press about the meeting. He followed up with appropriate personal and phone contacts. A memorandum that summarized information and recommendations was
sent to all members and to the press. Whenever possible, he continued to pass along information and to direct members of this group
to others with similar interests and vice versa.

Negotiation and Communication Tactics

Use of the methods of negotiation and communication involves
various tactics. In using negotiations, probes are made to find
possible negotiating alliances. When a potential group is found,
some stimulus for getting them to agree to negotiate is provided.
Later, bargaining takes place around the possible change and
who will do what. In using communication, information is provided that will stimulate a group to take some definite action.
A group may be confronted with information that points up
areas in which they need to act toward change. These and other
tactics are presented as a beginning repertoire. They are used as
an expedient to accomplish desired ends.

PROBE. Investigate, search, explore, ask questions. Ask for a
response that will put you in a better position to frame a subsequent request, to take a certain action, or to make a future
decision. The intent of the probe may include opening up a
dialogue or an avenue for communication, discovering the degree

of readiness and receptivity to change ideas, determining the availability of unused or untapped opportunities or resources, or ascertaining the nature of decision-making.

EXAMPLE

The community professional needed to make some decisions about how to work with a particular health agency. He called on the president of a voluntary organization that had successfully persuaded the reputedly uncooperative health agency to take over an important service. The community professional asked questions about what had happened and why they had been successful, whereas other groups had been unsuccessful.

PLANT SEED OR SUGGEST. Plant an idea, suggestion, or specific information with the hope that it will sprout and develop. Make statements or requests that suggest a direction, a course of action, or a desired response.

EXAMPLE

The community professional sent letters to several civic and social-action organizations explaining the dependence of older persons, in addition to other groups (youth, poor), on public transportation and his interest in reducing bus rates for older persons. The letter also explained that the bus service was requesting subsidy from the city government and, as such, was a public issue. He suggested that they take the responsibility for letting their respective city governments know what kind of transportation improvements such a subsidy should cover, and he urged that it include reduced bus rates for older persons.

BARGAIN. Reach a settlement on an issue or action by arriving at terms that are viewed as mutually agreeable or advantageous. You and the other party can expect to give or perhaps to give up something in order to get something else. This is an important tactic in carrying out negotiations.*

EXAMPLE

In negotiations regarding the establishment of a grocery-delivery service, the community professional met with the owner of the gro-

---

*Meyerson, Martin, and Banfield, Edward C.: *Politics, Planning and the Public Interest.* Glencoe, Illinois: The Free Press, 1955, p. 307.

cery store to agree upon (or bargain for) what responsibilities each would take in getting the service started, i.e. the grocer would contact the delivery man and work out the details of the service with him, after which the community professional would prepare and distribute a brochure to potential users of the service.

STIMULATE. Provide a stimulus that will motivate a person (or group) to react in a way that you see as favorable.

EXAMPLE

The community professional mentioned in his contacts with a women's club that the employment service for older people (which the community professional hoped to negotiate with them) was a new and different idea and probably would be received by their national organization with a great deal of excitement. As far as the community professional knew, it would be a first of its kind—a unique new program of which they could be justly proud.

CONSULT. Engage in problem finding or problem solving through the provision of specialized help around a particular area.

EXAMPLE

The coordinator of a new information, referral, and personal-services program for older people approached the community professional with a specific problem. The community professional had been involved continuously in the development of the program. Since the need for the service from its inception was greater than had been anticipated, the simple cumulative recording of the basics on each call had become unwieldy. Needed information on regular clients could not be easily retrieved, necessary compilation of statistics was time-consuming, and a categorization system by types of requests was needed for analysis and planning for the further development of the service. Because of his intimate knowledge of the program, the community professional was able to devise a workable record-keeping system in a minimum amount of time.

CONFRONT. Present information to others in a way that calls for a definite reaction on their part. This implies that you already know the stance or prior action of the group and that your view is at variance with their views or policies, either stated or inherent. It serves to sharpen the issue; it points up the consequences to which the current course is leading or has led.

As ordinarily used, the term confrontation carries implications of open anger and hostility. There is a high risk in using this tactic because, if he repeats it a few times, the community professional may lose the effectiveness achieved through use of his overall methods. One way of handling this problem is to structure differential roles for two community professionals. One can be abrasive while the other soothes hurt feelings.

Another approach is to view confrontation as a face-to-face meeting that is without negative affect on the part of the community professional. Do not enter a situation at the level of personalities except when doing such would be definitely advantageous.

Still another approach is to get other individuals or groups to make direct attacks on others when it appears more desirable for you to avoid doing so.

EXAMPLE

The community professional confronted key health services and decision makers with the need for a county-wide public health department, citing the positive consequences and impact that such a department could have on the lives of older persons and the negative impact caused by the lack of such services. He backed up his statement with a written report that provided his analysis and perspective concerning the obstructionist forces in the health sector of the community who had impeded the development of such a department. This paper stepped on a few toes, but it served to awaken the active interest of many potentially constructive forces within the health sector.

This action was taken only after the community professional had gained some measure of respect and recognition in the community as an authority on local problems of the aging. The "written report" route was taken when an analysis of health problems of the aging pointed toward the need for a total revision and examination of the public-health structure in the county. Provision by the community professional of information, analysis, and recommendation served as the first necessary step in this process.

AMELIORATE CONFLICT. Act in such a way as to diminish tensions that result from differing points of view. You may or may not be implicated directly in this conflict.

EXAMPLE

The community professional anticipated that conflict might arise between two organizations with whom he was separately negotiating for employment services for older people. When the conflict arose, he was prepared immediately to assure the two organizations that the change plans were both needed, that they were basically different, and that they were not in competition with each other.

SUPPORT AND REASSURE. Provide necessary supportive measures, such as morale building, handholding, and praise, in a manner that will enable an individual or group to move forward in a direction which will further a change idea or plan.

EXAMPLE

The community professional provided a great deal of encouragement, handholding, and subsequent praise to a very competent woman who agreed somewhat fearfully to assume leadership in organizing a senior-citizens' group in a rural area. This included speaking at the first meeting of the group, the offer of future assistance, much reassurance and praise, and follow-up contacts for reports on how the group was progressing.

INFORM. Give factual information that does not reflect your personal opinion or point of view.

EXAMPLE

The community professional presented some annotated research findings and social-provisions data to a neighborhood health clinic serving the poor, for their subsequent use in applying for a government grant. Based primarily on this information, their proposal included the poor elderly as one of their three major concerns.

ADVISE. Give information that includes your opinion or point of view, such as favoring one possible action over another.

EXAMPLE

The community professional met with a recreational department that was applying for a grant to improve services to older persons. Based on the social-provisions data, he suggested improvements in services that would reach elderly persons not now involved, rather than seconding their original plan to provide more services for those already using the program.

INTERNAL GUIDELINES FOR ACTION

As the community professional, you are finally out in the community where the task is to plan and create observable change— to make constructive things happen. How will you know if you are making things happen or whether events are moving in the right direction? This section presents some guidelines to help you to act effectively in achieving payoffs and end objectives.

Focus on Payoffs and Outcome

The realization of change plans most often occurs through a series of steps, i.e. finding a party willing to negotiate, negotiating the nature of the change plan and the commitments for tasks necessary in bringing about the plan, carrying out commitments. Completing such short-term payoffs marks progress toward realizing the intended change.

As a community professional, you must keep to the forefront what you have done, where you are, and where you are headed in bringing about payoffs and realizing the change plan. You must keep under surveillance whether or not a short-term step is, in actuality, a payoff toward fulfillment of an idea or plan.

What is being done tends to be measured in terms of activity and process, rather than in terms of accomplishments and outcomes. A focus on payoffs and outcomes represents a disciplined attempt to minimize the all-too-human tendency to correlate immediate activity with lasting results.

Safeguard Time

Time is the community professional's foundation for building change; it is his major contribution. Keeping track of this time helps to ensure its wise allocation and careful use. It indicates the amount of time and attention invested in a given line of activity.

Keeping careful track of time helps to relate and compare the time investments to payoffs and outcomes in terms of the significance of the predicted outcome. How would the time spent to achieve one thing compare to the time spent to achieve something else? Is the time invested worth the outcome? A time analysis along these lines is an important consideration in determining whether to continue, alter, add, or drop a line of activity.

Finally, keeping track of time helps to apportion time appropriately among the various lines of activity. How much time should be allocated to reach a certain payoff or outcome? Time is not really safeguarded and used wisely unless you also determine how much time you will give. Thus you not only keep track of time spent but you also allocate future time.

Keep Available and Use Important Information

Effective use of negotiations requires keeping track of the terms of the negotiations that are made in formal and informal bargaining sessions. This includes the following:

1. The major steps needed to bring about the change, e.g. finding a funding source.
2. The commitments all parties to the negotiation have made as to what each will do to fulfill the plan.
3. The details of the resulting plan, i.e. what the end product will be.
4. The progress being made toward the fulfillment of commitments.

Effective use of communication requires keeping track of all incoming and outgoing information and messages in a given area so that strategic use and control of the information is possible. You must be in a knowledgeable position to provide appropriate information, to recognize and use opportunistic situations as they arise, and to bring various groups together for mutually advantageous purposes.

Receive Feedback From Actions

Feedback is obtained when you identify the results of actions that are necessary to make adjustments and corrections in plans and actions. Acting in a community creates information about those actions that, in turn, serve as a new platform from which to regulate future planning and action.

EXAMPLE

Sometimes this feedback will be available immediately. The community professional arranges a meeting for the purpose of getting a group to enter negotiations around a certain idea. He keeps a record of eventful happenings at such a meeting.

At other times, the community professional needs to obtain the information. He may engage in actions that he hopes will result in an increased use of a certain service by a particular group of people. In order to assess the effectiveness of his actions, he needs to ask the agency for the necessary information.

This system of feedback and correction takes place as the following tasks are completed:

1. Plan actions and then predict the results of your actions.
2. Identify and then record your actions.
3. Take responsibility for getting the information necessary to determine the actual outcome of your actions (feedback).
4. Assess the action and the result of the action in terms of moving toward or reaching certain payoffs.
5. Make any necessary corrections, such as eliminating steps not leading toward a desired payoff, changing the group toward which communication is directed, changing the party to negotiations, eliminating or altering the plan or idea, or changing the methods or tactics.
6. Plan further action.

Make Rational Decisions

In making difficult decisions as rationally as possible, you need to consider such things as time and desired outcome; alternate change ideas, courses of action, and tactics; and the consequences of selecting a given alternative. These considerations are illustrated in the following questions:

1. Would choosing to pursue one change idea foreclose the possibility of also pursuing another idea?
2. Would using a certain tactic with a given group militate against negotiating with that group?
3. Would making a certain commitment channel all subsequent actions?

Be Accountable

As an employee who requires relative autonomy and works

independently, you must function in a manner that will permit the person or people representing your sponsoring body to be readily apprised of operations in any or all lines of activity. Thus, it is necessary to organize and disseminate information about your activities in an expedient manner.

A suggested structure for implementing a workable system for feedback, evaluation, and correction is detailed in Chapter 6.

FLEXIBILITY OF THE COMMUNITY PROFESSIONAL'S ROLE

In Chapter 2, the presentation of existing approaches for the community professional focused on a description of his methods and role. It also was pointed out that although the community professional uses the methods of negotiation and communication, his role is flexible. In any given situation, he may act as an advocate, an enabler, a change agent, a broker, and so forth. The role is determined by the nature of the situation, the relationship to the other party(s) to the negotiation or communication, and the outcome desired.

Except for the relationship with his sponsoring body, the community professional avoids becoming an integral part of formal or informal structures that require system maintenance or that inhibit him from taking action on his own. His role is to work with or on behalf of, rather than at the direction of, any group, and he is a participant in the decision-making that directs his work. The community professional attempts to bring about change by offering assistance.

Chapter 6

INTERNAL PROCEDURES FOR ACTION

T O bring about change effectively requires the community professional to keep track of (and on top of) a number of things, to assess and evaluate numerous events, and to make many decisions. This begins with sound record keeping that includes a system for feedback and correction and for filing information for ready access.

The system presented here provides the means to do the following:

- Achieve a sense of purpose and direction.
- Focus on payoffs and outcome.
- Safeguard time.
- Have readily available and use necessary information.
- Receive feedback from actions in order to assess actions and to plan future action.
- Make rational and feasible decisions.
- Be accountable.

The procedures involved are flexible, may be adapted as needed, and serve to reinforce the discipline necessary to function efficiently. Although they are presented here in sufficient detail to be helpful, the actual procedures take relatively little time. They permit the community professional to choose among different demands on his energy from day to day and to review each month the progress he has made toward selected short-term goals.

PROCEDURES FOR FEEDBACK AND CORRECTION

Forecast Sheets are prepared as the plan of action for a one-month period. During this action period, Journal Sheets are kept

71

on a daily, ongoing basis. At the end of the action period, about two days time is set aside to make assessments and to plan for the next action period. Review and Appraisal Sheets are completed based on information from the Forecast Sheets and Journal Sheets, as an assessment of the past action period. Then, based on this new assessment, Forecast and Time Tally Sheets are completed to expedite the next one-month period.

Evaluating and planning on a monthly basis is suggested, although the time span can be adapted to fit the number of community professionals employed and the scope of the effort.

Feedback and correction take place through the use of the following forms:

- Forecast Sheet (Fig. 1)
- Journal Sheet (Fig. 2)
- Review and Appraisal Sheet (Fig. 3)
- Time Tally Sheet (Fig. 4)

Mimeograph or duplicate an ample supply of these forms.

FORECAST SHEETS

Forecast Sheets (Figs. 5 and 6) are prepared for each line of activity and serve as the current plan of action (and referent for action) until the periodic assessment. Forecast Sheets include time allocations, proposed action, and anticipated payoffs.

Journal Sheets

Journal Sheets (Figs. 7 and 8) are a depository for recording all activities and outcomes. This includes decisions, actions, and results, in addition to preparation, thinking, and planning. Consistent and disciplined use of the Journal Sheets is necessary to organize day-by-day work, to ensure continuity of effort, and to facilitate reflective thought.

The importance of the Journal Sheets cannot be stressed enough. They provide the necessary base for all subsequent planning, action, and evaluation. They also provide a communication channel that enables two or more community professionals to keep each other immediately and accurately informed, since all recording is done on the same Journal Sheets.

FIGURE 1
FORECAST SHEET

Date: _____

Target Area: _____

Line of Activity: _____

Summary Notes on Decisions and Plans:

Time Span: _____
New Review Date: _____
Time Allocated: _____

Payoffs Forecasted:

Forecast Sheet Number: _____

FIGURE 2
JOURNAL SHEET

Target Area: _____

Line of Activity: _____

Initial	Date	Entry	Time Spent	Follow-up Notes

Journal Sheet Number: _____

FIGURE 3
REVIEW AND APPRAISAL SHEET

Target Area: _____

Date: _____

Line of Activity: _____

Summary: Notes and Findings

Time Span: _____
Time Spent: _____
Time Allocated: _____
Difference: (+) _____
        (−) _____

Payoffs Forecasted − Actual Payoff:

Review & Appraisal Sheet Number: _____

FIGURE 4
TIME TALLY SHEET

Time Span Reviewed _____ to _____   Time Allocation for Period _____ to _____

LINE OF ACTIVITY	A Allocated Time for Period _____ to _____	B Time Actually Spent During Period _____ to _____	C Difference Between A & B (+ or -)	D Time To Be Allocated Next Period _____ to _____
	hrs.	hrs.	hrs.	hrs.
TOTAL HOURS				

Time Available for Allocation

Time Spent Average: _____   Difference (estimated extra time to allocate): _____

Time To Be Allocated Total (D): _____   Time Tally Sheet Number: _____

FIGURE 5

EXAMPLE OF A COMPLETED FORECAST SHEET

ACTION ON AGING
Champaign County, Illinois

Date: 7/16/69

Target Area: Employment

Line of Activity: Senior Talent Employment Pool

Time Span: 7/16/69-8/15/69
New Review Date: 8/15/69
Time Allocated: 40 hours

Payoffs Forecasted

1. Number of returns of skill forms from older persons: 35.
2. Number of men recruited: 10.
3. Procurement of one definite funding source for 1st year: yes.
4. Completion of mechanics of operating service—forms and procedures: yes.
5. Number of Club K volunteers to participate in operation of services: at least 10 women.

Summary Notes on Decisions and Plans

1. Continue to work on commitment to recruit more older persons for the pool. More men are needed. Will work through Telecare (referrals and newsletter) and through news releases. If newspaper and radio releases don't bring good response, we will run an ad in the papers. We can afford a couple of these. Also plan to be on lookout for people who might be interested in paying for ads. Another alternative would be to work with the University retirement office. Nonacademic retirees might be a good source of interested men.

2. Examine and plan with Women's Club K around specific details or actual mechanics of setting up and coordinating S.T.E.P. Major concern will be that of making method practical for the volunteers so that their initial enthusiasm will not fade quickly. Our assistance will be primarily a consultative one. Problems to be worked out are (a) manning the telephone (having to stay home all day), (b) keeping all volunteers informed about the current employment status of each pool member and which older person an employer hired, and (c) plan for continued publicity and recruitment for the pool.

3. Seriously pursue a funding source. Leads are very limited. Some ideas are the United Way, service groups (especially Soroptimists, whose community-service effort is primarily giving money), civic groups (E Club—gerontology is national project), church groups, or groups of retired persons. Plan to do a lot of probing. Look through Community Agency and Organization File. This, along with number 2, will take most of the time allotted.

Forecast Sheet Number: 100

FIGURE 6

EXPLANATION OF ENTRIES ON FORECAST SHEET

[Identifying Information]   Date: _____

Target Area: _____

Line of Activity: _____

Time Span: [Inclusive Dates]
New Review Date: _____
Time Allocated: [Amount of time you are prepared to spend]

Summary Notes on Decisions and Plans
[Set down a summary of the major activities planned and the purpose of such activities. This would include major decisions regarding the future focus for activity and the particulars concerning possible alternatives and methods for implementing given alternatives.

One of the activities might be a meeting with Group X to probe for possible negotiations around a particular change idea. You would set down what steps might be taken if the group responded in one way and what steps might be taken if they responded in another way.
Appendix IV presents additional examples of Forecast Sheets.]

Payoffs Forecasted
[Enter the payoffs to be used for the next period and the predicted outcome. Payoffs are short-term steps directed at fulfilling an idea or change plan. They focus on outcome, rather than process, in order to provide the best indicators of progress toward realizing a plan or idea. Quantify as much as possible.]

Forecast   Sheet Number: _____

78

Make entries on the Journal Sheets chronologically by line of activity. Record the date of the activity or entry, appropriate or necessary details of the activity, the amount of time spent, and follow-up notes. Place materials that are the product of activity, such as letters or memorandums written or received, following the appropriate Journal Sheet (Figs. 9 and 10). If such materials are bulky or of minimal importance, record a cross-reference citation on the Journal Sheets and file elsewhere.

When change efforts begin, organize the Journal Sheets with only one general or miscellaneous line of activity for each target area. As one or more specific ideas develop with some potential for realization, organize the Journal Sheets by lines of activity under each target area.

The use of Journal Sheets must be efficient and functional. This means that regardless of whether there is a phone call, a meeting, or some hard thinking, the Journal Sheets need to be immediately accessible for entries. This is true whether you are in the field or at your office. Proper use of these sheets eliminates the often time-consuming process of later transferring information from pieces of scratch paper to the current form. Also the risk of lost or misplaced information is minimized.

FIGURE 7
EXAMPLE OF A COMPLETED JOURNAL SHEET

ACTION ON AGING
Champaign County, Illinois
Target Area: Employment

Line of Activity: S.T.E.P. (Senior Talent Employment Pool)

Initial	Date	Entry	Time Spent	Follow-up Notes
N.R. S.S.	7/25	Luncheon with Mrs. X, Mrs. D, and Mrs. S about the details of operating S.T.E.P. Showed them the brochure we've prepared for S.T.E.P. They liked it. Need a telephone number. Told them about inquiry into telephone answering services. Think they'll decide on Service B.	1½ hrs. x 2 = 3 hrs.	
		Mrs. X showed us sample forms—employer request form, pool member registration form, and pool member employment form (to keep track of employment). Decided on some revisions. She'll take responsibility for getting mass copies made.		
		Talked about screening applicants; can begin shortly. Mrs. X responsible for this. We'll continue to recruit more people, especially men.		
		Have about 7 volunteers. Need a couple more. Mrs. D will try to get more. Mrs. S has begun organizing them. Will work 1 or ½ day shift. Don't want to be tied to phones—perhaps they could call answering service periodically. Each volunteer needs complete file of information. How will volunteers keep information current? What about follow-up? Mrs. S and Mrs. D will work on this.		

80

S.S.	7/25	Prepared and mailed news release for the local papers for **S.T.E.P.** recruitment. Emphasized recruiting more men. Filed in Action File under News Releases, Employment.	1 hr.	
N.R.	7/25	Met with a friend, Mrs. A, who is on the Missions Commission of Broadmoor Methodist Church. Told her about S.T.E.P.—very interested. Also told her about financial need, particularly for telephone answering service. She said Commission has a yearly budget which includes allocation of funds for special purposes. Said she'd talk to the leader of the Commission, Mrs. R. Mrs. A questioned whether they could donate the $500 needed, but might be able to make some contribution. I asked her to let me know the response of this lady. She suggested we submit a written request for funds to the Commission.	45 min.	Check back in a week.
N.R.	7/26	Wrote a letter to above group requesting funds. (Carbon attached.)	2 hrs.	Mailed on 7/27. Copy filed in a new folder entitled "Correspondence on Funding for S.T.E.P."
S.S.	7/26	Wrote memorandum to Mrs. D, Mrs. X, and Mrs. S, re: details of operating S.T.E.P.—decisions made at 7/25 meeting, where development stands, what still needs to be done. (Carbon attached.)	2½ hrs.	Mailed 7/27. Copy filed in S.T.E.P. General Correspondence folder.
N.R.	7/27	Received call from Mr. Z who saw news release about S.T.E.P. He would like a skill form. Address is 304 Andrews Avenue, Urbana, phone: 984-9000.	5 min.	Have secretary send skill form. Sent 7/27.

N.R. S.S.	7/27	We talked at length about best possible funding sources for S.T.E.P.	2 hrs. x 2 = 4 hrs.	Get out letters. File carbons in Action File, Correspondence for Funding folder.
		Decided to send a letter or memo similar to that sent to the Broadmoor Methodist Church to several civic groups in the community. Revised letter.		
S.S.	7/27	Received skill form from 3 men—Mr. F, Mr. Z, Mr. W.		
N.R.	7/28	Called Mrs. X. Suggested to her that screening of S.T.E.P. applicants could begin. She said that if we turned over the skill return sheets to her, she would take responsibility for the screening. Told her we'd bring them to her office tomorrow. Will forward others as they come in.	15 min.	Talk to Mrs. X tomorrow.
S.S.	7/28	Mrs. B, Telecare Coordinator, called about further recruiting through Telecare client newsletter. See Telecare Sheet 105.	20 min.	Work on next week.

Journal Sheet Number: 120

FIGURE 8
EXPLANATION OF ENTRIES ON JOURNAL SHEET

[Identifying Information]
Target Area: _____

Line of Activity: _____

Initial	Date	Entry	Time Spent	Follow-up Notes
		[Include all information you may wish to retrieve at a later time; keep a time record of, or review for, evaluation. Make entries as the activities take place during the course of telephone calls, conferences and meetings, think sessions compiling a list of "things to do," and writing a letter or memo.		[Enter any reminders that activity may elicit. Use these to make notes to the secretary, place information on calendar, etc.]

The degree of detail entered depends on what occurred. For example, someone calls you. Enter the name, plus anything about the conversation that you think may be important. Jot down any reactions, thinking, observations, or planning. When in doubt about the amount of detail to include, err on the side of including too much until you have had some experience with using this system.

Use referencing and cross-referencing to simplify the process of keeping records. If you are writing a letter or memorandum, enter the fact that you are working on a particular letter and then place a copy in the binder attached to the appropriate Journal Sheet, or indicate where letter is filed. Make brief entries referring to letters and other pertinent information received. Indicate where these are filed. Cross-referencing (particularly in closely related or interrelated lines of activity) avoids or minimizes duplicate record keeping.]

Journal Sheet Number: _____

FIGURE 9
EXAMPLE OF LETTER FILED WITH JOURNAL SHEETS

ACTION ON AGING
United Community Council of Champaign County
303 South Wright Street
Champaign, Illinois 61820
356-3721

July 26, 1969

Mrs. R., Chairman
Missions Commission
Broadmoor Methodist Church
1515 West Alexander
Urbana, Illinois 61801

RE: Need for Financial Resources to Operate a Senior
Talent Employment Pool

Dear Mrs. R.:

Action on Aging is a special project of the United Community Council of Champaign County, designed to help agencies and organizations in the community increase, improve, or develop services for older persons in Champaign County. Since we have begun operating, we have been actively involved in developing a 24-hour telephone information and referral service which also provides several personal services to older persons, that otherwise do not exist, and several other services. In addition, we are currently involved in attempting to help develop a senior talent employment pool.

At the present time, there is almost no place in Champaign County to which older persons can turn if they want part-time, flexible employment. The reason for this is that the employment services which exist are geared mainly to providing full-time employees for ongoing businesses.

At the same time, there is little or no place to which homeowners or families, young or old, can turn for help with jobs around the home, such as carpentry, painting, landscaping, various fix-it jobs, baking, fixing sandwiches for a party, mending, babysitting, tutoring, sitting with pets while family goes on vacation, and many other jobs which are too small to be handled by larger companies or businesses.

Today, in Champaign County, the approximate minimum Social Security is $55.00 and the approximate maximum is $165.00 for those persons 65 years of age and over who retire at age 65. These figures are considerably less for persons who are often forced to retire at age 62. Older people, often fiercely independent and proud, may refuse to accept public assistance to supplement their Social Security despite the fact that they may be eligible for such funds.

Action on Aging feels that in addition to providing older persons with worthwhile employment opportunities, which could help supplement the limited income from Social Security or other retirement pensions, the services which this type of talent pool could provide would also meet a definite need in this community. In the end, the services which such a talent pool could offer will depend on the talents and skills of the older persons who make up the pool.

Women's Club K, whose national project for years has been concerned with aging persons, have graciously agreed to coordinate the employment talent pool if Action on Aging will recruit enough older persons to get the service off the ground. We have been actively involved in this and will soon reach the point of having enough older persons interested to begin the service. Women's Club K will operate the service on a volunteer basis out of their own homes, through the use of an answering service. However, an answering service and some necessary basic supplies will cost money.

Because the major fund raising activity of Women's Club K had to be cancelled this year, Action on Aging has agreed to assume responsibility for locating some financial resources. These resources would be used to assist with the operation of the senior talent employment pool service until such time as Women's Club K is able to provide the money for operating the service.

We have estimated that the major cost of operating the service for a year would come to approximately $450.00, with the answering service fee running approximatly $222.00 ($18.50 × 12 months) and the business phone running approximately $155.00 ($13.00 × 12 months). The remaining $73.00 would be used for other expenses such as paper, stamps, toll calls within the country, etc.

Mrs. A, a former member of the Commission, has indicated to us that you have an interest in local services which meet definite community needs and have shared in these services through your financial support.

We are asking you to share in this service by providing an initial contribution to Women's Club K. It is anticipated that the need for financial assistance for Club K will be temporary, probably only during the first year of operation. If adequate funding can be located, the service is set to start in the early fall.

We would be happy to talk with you further about this matter if your group is interested in making some financial commitment in helping this much-needed service get underway.

Sincerely,
(Mrs.) Naomi Rempe
(Mrs.) Suzy Small

NR/SS/vmt

FIGURE 10
EXAMPLE OF A MEMORANDUM FILED WITH JOURNAL SHEETS

TO: Women's Club K, Mrs. X, Mrs. D, Mrs. S.
FROM: Action on Aging, Naomi Rempe and Suzy Small
DATE: August 4, 1969
RE: Details of Operating the Senior Talent Employment Pool

In order to clarify for all of us the decisions reached in our meeting of July 25, 1969, we would like to present our picture of where the development of S.T.E.P. stands at present.

An agreement has been reached that enough older persons have returned their skill forms to warrant moving ahead in making definite plans to start the service. We will still continue to recruit more elderly persons, since there is a definite need for more men.

According to Mrs. S, about 7 Women's Club K members, in addition to herself and Mrs. D, have volunteered for telephone duty. Mrs. D has agreed to recruit a few more. There are advantages to starting the service with a small number of volunteers, at least until any major problems are worked out. However, we know you share our concern that this effort should not become a burden. This is the fastest way to lose good volunteers.

Screening of applicants for the pool can begin shortly. Mrs. X has agreed to handle this. It's going to be a big job and additional volunteers might be needed. We're sure Mrs. X understands this whole process much better than we do.

Another point of discussion at the meeting was the telephone answering service. There are only two in this community, but we suggest using Service B because it is more reasonably priced. The cost for this service will come to about $31.50 a month. You will need to make some decision about whether to use this service. We will be happy to make the arrangements, in Women's Club K's name, of course.

This brings us to another point, namely, funding. Approximately $180.00 has been raised so far. We have agreed to continue working on this until the service starts. As you know, we have a listing of many organizations that could be contacted. However, if you have any bright ideas, please let us know.

There are many procedural details for which decisions must be made. Through all of our discussion at the meeting, the following decisions were made:

1. Mrs. X will revise the forms necessary to operate the service and will take responsibility for mimeographing these. The registration form will be completed with the screening. All volunteers should have complete information on all members of the pool.

2. Volunteers will work a day shift or a half-day shift. If it's okay with the answering service, volunteers will call them periodically through-

out the day, rather than be called as each call comes to the answering service.

3. Although no decision was made as to how to keep each volunteer's records current on such things as when, how, and by whom, pool members are being employed, Mrs. S and Mrs. D agreed to take responsibility for working on this.

There are still actions which need to be taken or decisions which need to be made.

1. Setting a definite time to begin the service. There seems to be a tentative agreement that it will be in the early fall, but a definite date needs to be set.

2. Making plans for continued publicity. We are willing to make up a large quantity of the brochure we showed you and do some distributing. We will give you a large quantity of these for you to distribute also. We'll give you a list of the areas or organizations we've covered so that the distribution will not be duplicated. However, the decision as to who will take responsibility for other forms of publicity (once the date is set and telephone number procured), both initially and after the service is underway, must be made. We suggest that you start seeking a Women's Club K volunteer, perhaps a person not interested in the telephone aspect of the service. In addition to publicity about the service, there will also be a need for ongoing recruitment.

We will be happy to meet again. Other problems which have not come to your or to our attention will undoubtedly arise.

Review and Appraisal Sheets

Review and Appraisal Sheets (Figs. 11 and 12) provide a method to do the following:

1. Appraise where the line of activity is heading.

2. Appraise the nature and degree of commitments made.

3. Appraise and compare payoffs and courses of action.

4. Review and summarize past events in view of past forecasts.

This sheet is designed to summarize and assess the work of the action period for each line of activity. It shows action taken, time invested, and payoffs achieved.

The Journal Sheets and the previous Forecast Sheets are the source of information from which the summary and assessment are made.

FIGURE 11

EXAMPLE OF A COMPLETED REVIEW AN APPRAISAL SHEET

ACTION ON AGING
Champaign County, Illinois   Date: 8/16/69
Target Area: Employment   Line of Activity: Senior Talent Employment Pool

Time Span: 7/16/69-8/15/69
Time Spent: 55 hours
Time Allocated: 40 hours
Difference: (+) 15 hours
(−)

Summary: Notes and Findings

1. Commitment made to help with initial fund-raising is substantially fulfilled.

   a. Made use of an opportunistic situation to raise funds for S.T.E.P.—organized, with help of Mrs. S from Club K, the participation of Club K members and their friends in a telephone research project. Raised approximately $180.

   b. Received a lead that the Missions Commission of Broadmoor Methodist Church might be interested in contributing financially to S.T.E.P. Wrote a formal request to them on behalf of Women's Club K for funds. Received a reply that they would contribute $50.00.

   c. Sent letters of request for S.T.E.P. funds, similar to that sent to Broadmoor Methodist Church, to 20 civic groups in the community. Have, as yet, received no replies, positive or negative. We still anticipate some response.

Payoff Forecasted—Actual Payoff

1. Number of returns of skill forms from older persons (35 total) = 43.

2. Number of men recruited (10) = 8.

3. Procurement of definite funding sources for 1st year (good potential for "yes") = procured $230 out of approximately $450 needed or about 50%.

4. Completion of mechanics of operating service—forms and procedures (yes) = yes, about complete.

5. Number of volunteers to participate in operation of service (10) = 2 coordinators and 9 women so far.

2. The two coordinators of S.T.E.P., Mrs. S and Mrs. D have become actively involved. We have met and talked often with Mrs. X and them about actual mechanics of setting up and co-ordinating S.T.E.P.

   a. Revised initial record-keeping forms and system for S.T.E.P. which Mrs. X drew up.

   b. They've recruited enough volunteers to start service and have made the major decisions as to how volunteers will operate.

   c. Agreed with Club K's plan to start S.T.E.P. on Sptember 2, 1969.

   d. We revised and made up large quantities of attached S.T.E.P. brochures for community distribution. Did some distributing.

   e. Drew up list of other organizations to whom brochures could be given. Women's Club K agreed to assume responsibility for further distributing. We'll help if time permits.

   f. Mrs. X agreed to take the responsibility for publicity once service started.

   g. Contracted for business telephone and answering service in name of Club K.

3. Continued, through news media, to recruit actively more men in order to have a better male-female ratio for S.T.E.P.

4. With the above activities, we have virtually completed our commitments to them, except for more help in initial publicity and following through on any responses to past fund-raising overtures.

89

Review & Appraisal Sheet Number: 138

FIGURE 12

EXPLANATION OF ENTRIES ON REVIEW AND APPRAISAL SHEET

[Identifying Information]   Date: _____
Target Area: _____

Line of Activity: _____

Summary: Notes and Findings

Time Span: [Inclusive Dates]
Time Spent: _____
Time Allocated: _____
Difference: (+) _____
            (−) _____

[Summarize significant happenings since last forecast, including progress on decisions and plans set down in last Forecast Sheet.

List commitments made.

Review where you are and where the other party is in fulfilling commitments.

Evaluate where the line of activity is and where it's going in terms of the change plans or ideas. Are the fulfillment of certain plans or ideas and the more immediate payoffs worth the amount of time spent?

Consider possible future actions or steps in the light of where the line of activity stands now.

Appendix IV presents additional examples of Review and Appraisal Sheets.]

Payoffs Forecasted—Actual Payoff

[List the payoffs as they appeared in the last Forecast Sheet. Then enter the actual payoff: what, in fact, was achieved since the last forecast. (Put forecasted payoffs in parenthesis to differentiate them from actual payoffs). Separate by a dash.]

[Time Spent (above): Enter the total obtained from the Time Spent column in the Journal Sheets. Time Allocated (above): Enter time allocated in last Forecast Sheet.]

Review & Appraisal Sheet Number: _____

90

Time Tally Sheets

The decision to pursue a line of activity is made by conscious choice. (Lines are not all begun at one time but rather emerge at various points). One of the key factors in this choice is time. A time-based assessment of all lines of activity is important in the decision to pursue new lines of activity. This is not the same as a rigid time study of total work hours. Rather, it serves as a helpful guide in determining the following:

1. How much time is being spent on all the existing lines of activity?

2. Approximately how much of your time will be required in order to work toward fulfilling a change plan or idea?

3. How much time is there available to pursue a new line of activity?

Using hours as a base, the Time Tally Sheet (Fig. 13) pulls together the information needed for current evaluation and future planning of overall actions. It is filled out following the completion of the Review and Appraisal Sheets and the Forecast Sheets each month. Examination and analysis of the Time Tally Sheets may lead to a reappraisal of the time allocated to various lines of activity on the new Forecast Sheets or to the addition of a new line(s) of activity.

The evaluative assessments made and the comparison of the forecasted and actual payoffs permits you to obtain successively more accurate estimates in predicting time allocations for future action.

FIGURE 13
EXAMPLE OF A COMPLETED TIME TALLY SHEET

ACTION ON AGING
Champaign County, Illinois
Time Span Reviewed 7/16/69 to 8/15/69

Time Allocation for Period 8/16/69 to 9/15/69

LINE OF ACTIVITY	A Allocated Time for Period 7/16 to 8/15	B Time Actually Spent During Period 7/16 to 8/15	C Difference Between A & B (+ or −)	D Time To Be Allocated Next Period 8/16 to 9/15
	hrs.	hrs.	hrs.	hrs.
Grocery Delivery	2	Line Dropped		
Telecare	15	7	− 8	12
S.T.E.P.	40	55	+15	25
Public Employment Service	6	3	− 3	2
Sitter Service	10	11	+ 1	13
Home-Health-Help				
Miscellaneous	5	7	+ 2	5
County Senior Citizens	15	25	+10	10
Transportation	20	15	− 5	20
Medical Social Service	New Line			25
TOTAL HOURS	113	123	+12	112

Time Available for Allocation

Time Spent Average: 5/15 to 8/16 = 125

Difference (estimated extra time to allocate): 8/16 to 9/15 = 13 hours.

Time To Be Allocated Total (D): 8/16 to 9/15 = 112

Time Tally Sheet Number: 8

92

The following explains the entries on the Time Tally Sheet (Fig. 13).

Time Span Reviewed. Enter dates reviewed in the current Review and Appraisal Sheets.

Time Allocation for Period. Enter dates for which the current Forecast Sheets were completed.

Line of Activity. List all the lines of activity being pursued.

(Column A) Allocated Time for Period ———— *to* ————.
Enter dates of the last action period in column heading. List the amount of time that was allocated for each activity.

(Column B) Time Actually Spent During Period ———— *to* ————. Enter dates of the last action period in column heading. List the amount of time that actually was spent for each activity.

(Column C) Difference Between A and B (+ or —). Enter time difference between time allocated (A) and time spent (B).

(Column D) Time Allocated for Next Period ———— *to* ————.
Enter dates of next action period in column heading. List amount of time being allocated for the next action period.

Time Available for Allocation.

Time Spent Average. This is determined by averaging the total Time Actually Spent for the last three months (Column B). Total work hours during any given period are not used as a base referent because there is no attempt to carry out a total-time study of all work hours on a continuing basis. The time-based assessment is designed to account for blocks of time spent on the lines of activity. The total Time Actually Spent for just the last period (Column B) is not used because no one month is typical.

Time To Be Allocated Total. This refers to the total in Column D.

Difference. This refers to the difference between Time Spent Average and Time To Be Allocated Total (D). This difference will reflect the estimated extra time available for allocation or redistribution for the next time period, or it will indicate the amount of time overextended. If the available time is redistributed among the lines of activity already forecasted, the Time Allocated on the Forecast Sheets will have to be appropriately revised. In addition, the Time Tally Sheet must then be revised to show the corrected allocations.

Organizing Record-Keeping Forms

Keep Journal Sheets (completed and blank), completed Review and Appraisal Sheets, and Forecast Sheets in lightweight, colored plastic 3-ring binders (Fig. 14). Use a different-color binder for each target area. Use looseleaf dividers to separate lines of activity. Keep the Time Tally Sheets in a separate binder.

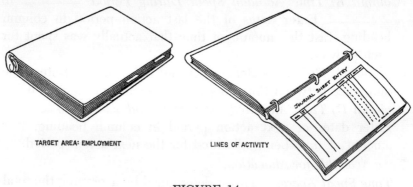

TARGET AREA: EMPLOYMENT   LINES OF ACTIVITY

FIGURE 14
ILLUSTRATION OF BINDERS USED TO HOLD
RECORD-KEEPING FORMS

For each line of activity, place the completed Review and Appraisal Sheets and Forecast Sheets behind the last Journal Sheet for the action period being reviewed and before a supply of blank Journal Sheets to be used during the next action period. If the last Journal Sheet is Sheet Number 54, the Review and Appraisal Sheet will be 55, the Forecast Sheet will be 56, and the next Journal Sheet will be 57. Number these regular forms consecutively for each separate line of activity. Ancillary materials attached to the Journal Sheets, such as copies of letters sent or received and memorandums written, are not included in this numbering system.

If a binder becomes too bulky, remove the earliest materials to a folder, and file behind the appropriate line of activity in the Action File. Forms from lines of activity that have been completed or dropped should be removed also and kept in a separate file.

The use of the flexible binders and this method of organizing these forms provides the necessary accessibility and mobility.

PROCEDURES FOR ORGANIZING RELATED INFORMATION

Action Worksheets

The Action Worksheets are a series of written summary accounts of the information gathered about different problem situations or areas for development in the selected life arena. They also serve as a record of the community professional's analysis of what and who could bring about change, and how this might best be accomplished.

Chapter 4 presented an outline for organizing information and ideas into Action Worksheets that serve as the background from which target areas and lines of activity are selected. In addition, the Action Worksheets are active reference sources for information and ideas from which strategic action is taken.

The categories in the outline for Action Worksheets are as follows:

1. Problem situation within the life arena.
2. Nature and extent of the problem situation.
   a. Nonlocal.
   b. Local.
3. Existing services dealing with the problem.
4. Change aids.
   a. Potential service resources.
   b. Program ideas.
   c. Groups.
   d. Laws.
   e. Funds.
5. Possible changes.
6. Potential lines of activity: alternative options for change.

Just as the record-keeping forms presented are the key sources for information about the community professional's actions, necessary for evaluation and planning, the Action Worksheets are the key source for life arena information and change aids. This is illustrated by Appendix III, which is an actual Action Worksheet on employment in the aging area. It was prepared in 1968-1969 using the six categories presented above. In addition to the summary, reference is often made to information found outside the Action Worksheet.

Completion of Action Worksheets is dependent on the gathering of information about the life arena as discussed in Chapter 3. The efficient completion of the Action Worksheets depends on how well the information gathered has been organized; therefore, a method of organizing this information into workable files is presented next.

Resource Files

The filing of information determines the usefulness of that information to the community professional's change efforts. The method for organizing resource files that is presented here should, of course, be adapted and individualized.

The minimal equipment needed in this filing system includes at least one or two four-drawer, standard-size file cabinets; standard-size file dividers; many manila folders; a one- or two-drawer, desk-top file cabinet designed to hold 4 x 6 in. filecards; and a bookshelf.

COMMUNITY AGENCY AND ORGANIZATION FILE. The Community Agency and Organization File contains information about community individuals, agencies, and groups that can be helpful. Include the names, addresses, and brief pertinent information about groups and people in the community who can be viewed as existing or potential change aids. Also use as a resource for compiling specialized mailing lists.

EXAMPLE

In fulfilling the commitment made to Women's Club K in begining the Senior Talent Employment Pool, the community professional attempted to obtain funds by contacting, through letters, civic organizations and women's clubs. The secretary used the Community Agency and Organization File to compile a mailing list of the presidents of these organizations.

Place the information on 4 x 6 in. cards (Fig. 15) and house in a desk-top file box for immediate access. On the lower, right-hand corner of the card, indicate the date (preferably in pencil) the card is made and when information is updated. You will then know how recently the information was entered.

FIGURE 15
COMMUNITY AGENCY AND ORGANIZATION FILE CARD

Public Employment Service (local) 809 North Atkins Street Champaign, Illinois 61820 982-7616	EMPLOYMENT

Manager: Mrs. Jane D., phone ext. 36
Assistant: Mrs. Alice B., phone ext. 15
(handles most older clients)

See: Regional Public Employment Office card   4/68

Place long listings, such as all the ministers and/or churches in the county, in a manila folder with a reference card in the desk-top file indicating where the longer list can be found (Action File, local change-aid category).

The categories of agencies and organizations will be determined by the nature of the life arena. The list of categories would include the following:
- Agencies, by type, and including personnel and boards.
- Governmental bodies and persons, including state and national congressmen.
- Mass media.
- Social action organizations.
- National, state, or regional organizations pertinent to the life arena (e.g. National Council on Aging, National Associa-

tion of Retired Persons, State Commission on Aging) and organizations that are potential change aids.

- Groups or individuals with special interest in the life arena (could be broken down further).
- Service and civic organizations.
- Women's clubs, including sorority alumnae.
- Doctors.
- Lawyers.
- Churches or ministers.
- Special interest groups.
- Health organizations.
- Educational organizations.
- Unions.

Information sources for this file include health and welfare directories, chambers of commerce, newspapers, and the yellow pages in the telephone book. Begin developing this file as you collect information on the local life arena as detailed in Chapter 3. This file must be kept current. Clip from the newspaper and update on the file card the news items that have to do with such things as election of new officers for the coming year, an added hospital board member, or the formation of a new social action organization. Continued contacts in the community will supply other information for this file.

NEWSPAPER CLIPPINGS FILE. Creating a working file of newspaper clippings is a challenge that, if met, can contribute greatly to your overall effectiveness. Clip and file, on an ongoing basis, selected articles related to the life arena and the local community and any articles indicating possible change aid potential.

Information found in newspapers that will be helpful to you are determined by the following:

1. *The life arena.* Information on housing could be important for the arena of aging, but it could have minimal importance if the arena were high school dropouts.
2. *Your own ideas.* What is seen as a potential change aid by one community professional may have no meaning for an-

other. For example, one community professional working in the arena of aging might view an article describing a youth-power employment program as a potential change idea that could be adapted for older persons. Another would see little value in the article for older persons.

3. *Size of the community and its newspapers and the time and money available to engage in this activity.* The larger and more extensive the newspaper(s), the more selective the clippings will need to be.

In developing a newspaper clipping file system, include the following areas:

1. *General community, state, and national:* major developments that may have great impact at the local level.

EXAMPLE

An article concerning state legislative action regarding the one-man, one-vote ruling for county government was clipped because of its potential impact on the local County Board of Commissioners.

2. *Information relating directly to the selected life arena:* special services, special events, meetings of organizations, general information about the arena, community issues, and change in the arena and/or directly concerning the life arena.

EXAMPLE

The community professional clipped articles about the local Social Security Administration that indicated an increase or decrease in the number of people served by type of benefit. Information from a specific article indicating that approximately 95 percent of the eligible elderly population were covered by Medicare was incorporated in in idea presented to the local bus company. The community professional suggested that elderly persons show their Medicare card to receive reduced bus rates.

3. *Community services:* social, health, and welfare services. Categorize further by type of service. Eliminate those with no relevance to the life arena, e.g. information on an adoption agency if the selected life arena is aging. Keep in mind that these services need not have potential for service to the

selected arena in the traditional sense, e.g. information on a children's home that may have relevance for special employment or volunteer opportunities for the elderly. Include articles that explain the function or purpose of the agency and changes which are taking place.

EXAMPLE

An article regarding the planned development of a nutrition aid program by the university home-economics extension led the community professional to contact the director of the program about informing the aides in training regarding the existence of a grocery delivery service for the aged and the handicapped. The community professional briefly spoke at one training session and distributed brochures about the grocery delivery service.

4. *Organization:* distinguished from agencies by the fact that agencies usually have paid staff and provide a direct service to some client group. Use to compile and update the Community Agency and Organization File. Place articles of this type in the Newspaper Clippings File if it is not convenient to enter complete information on the cards as to funding, purpose, special projects, etc.

EXAMPLE

An article on the purpose of a newly formed hospital planning council was used when the community professional sent a letter to all members of that group presenting the need for medical social services, which related very closely to one of their expressed purposes. The same article was later used by the community professional in an analysis of the health situation for older persons that included specific recommendations to that organization. This analysis and recommendations were then strategically distributed. Members of this organization listed in the article were placed in the Community Agency and Organization File.

5. *Money:* public and philanthropic. Include expenditure or budgeting of public money from bodies potentially relevant to change efforts, e.g. local public health department. Also include philanthropic expenditures and final reports of funds raised.

EXAMPLE

Articles on the donations of local civic, service, and social organizations were kept. When the community professional was seeking funds to help a special service get started, the secretary was instructed to go through this category and eliminate from her mailing list those smaller organizations that had recently made substantial donations for community betterment.

If the community professional is considering engaging in activities which will require community participation in terms of money, he should know where the local money is going. He should keep a newspaper file on voluntary donations and gifts. Who is giving the money, to whom, and how much? What kinds of programs are the voluntary and civic groups supporting? Different causes may be popular at different times. Knowledge about the giving trends may be important to action efforts attempted.

Build upon the categories presented. Revise your categories as necessary. You or a secretary can clip articles each day and immediately drop the articles into manila folders that are clearly marked by categories and subcategories.

LIFE ARENA INFORMATION FILE. The community professional needs to be knowledgeable about what has and what is currently going on in the selected life arena across the nation and in the state.

In addition to reviewing the literature, subscribe to appropriate national magazines and request placement on the mailing lists of national public and private organizations dealing with problems of, and programs for, the selected life arena. Stay informed on national and state legislative activities relevant to the arena through organizations providing such information. Request additional information about programs and studies currently being conducted. This should begin as soon as you start to study the life arena.

These magazines and materials provide a constant flow of information about program and change ideas, current areas of need and concern, potential service resources, and ideas about potential solutions to problems that can be used in planning and change efforts.

Information about what is currently happening across the nation may provide the germ for a change idea that may later be negotiated into a change plan.

EXAMPLE

Information from several sources on successful employment programs throughout the United States for older people influenced the selection of employment as a feasible target area around which some significant changes could be attempted. Descriptions of other programs were used in drawing up ideas about, and later developing the details for, a senior talent employment pool.

In the role of communicator, such information can be used in a planned or opportunistic way to bring about desired change.

EXAMPLE

The community professional provided information on the health problems and service needs of older persons to a newly formed free health center to help them in applying for funds to expand their service. As a result, the clinic assigned special priority for expanding services to the elderly in their grant request.

Organize the Life Arena Information File into several major categories, i.e., literature review, periodicals, and specific areas relating to the life arena. Use a separate category for notes on the literature review because many areas might be covered in one book or article. Keep a separate folder on bibliographic listings. File periodicals in a second category by title, since they usually contain information on numerous topics. With accurate and appropriate reference to these two categories in the Action Worksheets, information on a particular problem area or topic can easily be located.

Place in the category of specific areas relating to the arena, information received on nonlocal program ideas, funds, etc., for any given area (e.g., housing, employment, health, or recreation), having to do with the life arena.

At the beginning of the Life Arena Information File, keep a folder for correspondence dealing with materials and publications ordered. Store information too bulky for a filing cabinet on an appropriately marked bookshelf.

PLANNING FILE. In preparing for action, much information is compiled relating directly to change efforts in the community, such as formal or informal studies of the local life arena (Chapter 3), the community review (Chapter 3), Action Worksheets (Chapter 4), and any materials evolving from the process of selecting target areas (Chapter 4). This information also needs to be filed for ready reference.

EXAMPLE

Information on the social provisions study concerning employment, housed in the Planning File, was used in a letter presenting the need for a flexible employment service to the Women's Club K.

Organize the file by major categories, such as those listed above with further breakdown of categories as appropriate.

The first category, that of information on the local life arena, is further broken down by areas suggested in the informal study, presented in Chapter 3. They are as follows:

1. Social facts.
2. Problems and issues. Further categorize by type.
3. Proposed solutions: services and programs operating. Further categorize by type.
4. Information from people in life arena.
5. Information from local experts.
6. Public opinion. Include here notes on reactions and information about the arena elicited from community review interviews.

If your study of the local life arena included a more formal study, such as a social provisions study, the categories used in the study should also be used in the breakdown of the major category on information about the local arena.

Use the information in this category in completing Action Worksheets for ongoing planning and in negotiating and communicating.

EXAMPLE

Information housed in the Planning File on the population breakdown of Champaign County residents, age 60 and over, was used in telephone conversations with the local recreation department. Their staff was preparing a grant request to expand their services for the elderly. Later, a memorandum setting down specific population information requested was sent.

In the second major category, that of the community review, house the information in manila folders using headings such as interviews, drafts of analysis, written document, new information. More than one copy of the written document should be made.

The folder on new information is necessary because of the need to keep current on the functioning of the local community. Updating interviews may be indicated from time to time. Use the information kept in this folder to revise the written document, as necessary.

Throughout change efforts, use the community review as an aid in planning.

EXAMPLE

As change efforts began, those findings of the community review that showed some negative feelings on the part of the community people toward the University played an important part in the decision to emphasize the community professional's sponsorship by the Community Council and deemphasize its close association with the University.

File Action Worksheets by the problem area they cover. Since it is suggested that more than one copy of each be made, keep a separate folder on each Action Worksheet problem area.

Action Worksheets can be a source of information about a problem area for internal and external use. Be careful about direct use of them in change efforts, since subjective opinions are included.

EXAMPLE

The community professional gave a copy of an Action Worksheet dealing with health to a local public health physician. This was used by the physician in social action efforts to improve public health services. The community professional, however, gave the physician careful instructions as to the partially subjective nature of the Action Worksheet. The physician agreed to use the information carefully and not to cite the Action Worksheet publicly.

Keep the Action Worksheets that cover areas other than those selected as target areas. The opportunity to use them will undoubtedly arise. They will be an invaluable planning resource when you are giving consideration to new target areas or lines of activity.

Another category on miscellaneous planning materials would include materials prepared by you and others who assisted in the selection of the target areas. Further breakdown of this category is determined by the nature of the materials included. The information in this file can also be used in the decision to begin new target areas or lines of activity.

EXAMPLE

When time to engage in a new line of activity became available, the community professional used information that had been compiled and not used on potential target areas and lines of activity to present some alternatives to the advisory group. The decision was made to engage in a line of activity having to do with transportation.

ACTION FILE. Memorandums, letters, news media releases, speeches, and local incoming correspondence are an integral part of the action effort. File these by target areas with further categorization by lines of activity.

An additional copy of the most pertinent materials can be attached to the appropriate Journal Sheet, especially if copy facilities are readily available. If not, file the materials in the Action File with appropriate cross-reference in the Journal Sheets. If possible, duplicate materials from the Planning File that are directly pertinent to a given line of activity so that they can also be placed, as appropriate, in the Action File. For example, a copy of the Action Worksheet on employment and a summary copy of the social provisions study results having to do with employment also were placed in the Action File.

New lines of activity are added and others are dropped. Information in the Action File and in the record-keeping binders on those lines of activity that have been dropped are pulled and housed in a separate miscellaneous file.

Aside from filing by target area and lines of activity, include in the Action File a separate category for local change aids. This category is a separate one in the file because the information it includes may be applicable to several lines of activity.

EXAMPLE

A listing of all the mass media in the county, i.e. radio, television, and newspapers, was kept. The listing sheet was followed by an explanation of how these media could be used, particularly radio and television stations. The explanations included a listing of ongoing programs devoted in whole or in part to community issues and information. The community professional frequently used this information for publicity purposes. In addition, since mimeographed copies were made, the community professional often assisted community groups and individuals by providing them with this information.

Further divide the change aid category, using a breakdown similar to that listed for the Action Worksheets. The subheading of potential service resources includes available brochures describing local services, agencies, or organizations. The subheading on groups includes the longer listings, such as doctors or churches, cross-referenced in the Community Agency and Organization File.

Chapter 7

TASK CHART FOR THE
COMMUNITY PROFESSIONAL

I N the preceding chapters, an attempt has been made to assist the reader in the many facets involved in the community professional's efforts to create positive change. These activities and procedures are presented here in chart form so that a total overview of the Bilateral Planning and Action Approach can be seen.

TASK CHART FOR THE COMMUNITY PROFESSIONAL

Sequential Steps	Approx. Time	Pertinent Information	Procedural Considerations	Conclusions and Decisions
A. Obtain information necessary for action.	1 to 2 months	*Areas to be Covered* Problems and issues. Problem situations existing in the life arena.	Review literature, census materials, research studies.	
1. An overview of the life arena.			Get as many substantiating facts as possible.	
		Social facts. Primary social, psychological, environmental, economic and demographic characteristics.	Try to get an overall picture rather than concentrating efforts on one or two problems. Obtain statistics which are major indicators of people, problems, and ideas in the life arena.	
		Proposed solutions. Results of attempt to improve conditions.		
		Voice of the people. What the people in the arena think, say, and do about their own problems.	Do not rely on one person's point of view.	
		Voice of the experts. What the experts say about the life arena and problems.	Subscribe to appropriate national magazines. Place name on mailing lists of public and private organizations dealing with problems of and programs for the life arena, including legislative activity. Request additional informa-	
		Public opinion. What society thinks about the life arena.		

Sequential Steps	Approx. Time	Pertinent Information	Procedural Considerations	Conclusions and Decisions
		Underlying social values. Values demonstrated in prior helping attempts.	tion about programs and studies. Retain in a manner which allows easy and continued accessibility.	Identify those areas and situations for which local information will be sought.
2. The local life arena.	1 to 2 months	*Areas to be Covered*	Begin developing Life Arena Information File.	
		Problems and issues. Local indicators or manifestations of problem conditions in life arena.	Review local studies and census materials.	
		Social facts. Descriptive identification of people in local life arena.	Gather local information through informal means or through formal research procedures. Both require widespread community contact.	
			Direct questioning as well as observations are required.	
		Proposed solutions. How much of what kind of services are being provided to help understand, deal with, or alleviate the problem situations identified.	Subscribe to local newspapers. Clip appropriate articles. Develop Newspaper Clipping File.	

Sequential Steps	Approx. Time	Pertinent Information	Procedural Considerations	Conclusions and Decisions
		Voice of the people. What people in the local life arena think, say, and do about their own problems. Do they see any recourse for these problems?	Begin developing Community Agency and Organization File, Planning File, and that section of the Action File dealing with local change aids.	
		Voice of the experts. What leaders working on behalf of the local life arena are thinking and doing.		Selection of problem conditions which should be explored as potential areas for change.
		Public opinion. What the community thinks about the life arena. Is the life arena valued?		
3. How the local community functions — a community change review.	2 to 4 weeks	*Areas to be Covered*	Begin review through an interview with someone who is well acquainted with the community.	
		Process of change.	Use a "working referral" system (asking person to recommend others, etc.). Continue the study.	
		Major changes which have taken place in last 5 years, are currently underway, or are being planned — who, what, when, how?		

110

Sequential Steps	Approx. Time	Pertinent Information	Procedural Considerations	Conclusions and Decisions
		Issues and problems in community change efforts, successful and unsuccessful.	Approximately 15-20 interviews are needed.	
		Common change patterns (both formal and informal) used in bringing about change, as well as differences, complexities, etc.	In addition to studying the metropolitan area, select sample of rural communities for study.	
		Community leadership. Who are the opinion shapers and how do they operate?	Analyze review and compile this information on the community in a usable manner, i.e. a written document. Place information in the Planning File.	
		Issues and problems in health and welfare.		
		Historical community perspective. Factors significant to change efforts.		Identification of patterns upon which change efforts might be focused or ideas about how the community professional might best operate.
B. Translate information into action.	1 to 2 weeks (a culminating activity resulting from work to date)	*Selection of working stance, (overall direction for creating change) is influenced by*	Analysis of this information often suggests potential working stances in conflict with each other.	

111

Sequential Steps	Approx. Time	Pertinent Information	Procedural Considerations	Conclusions and Decisions
1. Select a working stance for further planning and action.		Prevalent public opinion about people in life arena and their problems.	When such conflicts appear, become as knowledgeable as possible and then make thoughtful, arbitrary decisions.	Selection of a working stance: spelling out the broad "who, what, and how," of the change efforts. Defining what is desirable and indicating an avenue for moving in this direction.
		What people in arena see as desirable.	After conflicts are resolved, there may remain two or more philosophically compatible working stances to choose from.	
		What community professional sees as desirable for people in life arena.		
		Manner in which problems in life arena reflect problems in society.	Not a systematic formula, but an aid to conscious consideration of alternate directions toward which change efforts can be directed in terms of benefits to people in the arena.	
		Result of local efforts and attitudes on life of people in the arena.		Selection made by community professional and his sponsoring body.
		Effect of national programs on life of people in arena.		

112

Sequential Steps	Approx. Time	Pertinent Information	Procedural Considerations	Conclusions and Decisions
		Current thinking and research in field as to what is desirable.		This will direct the focus of target areas selected and changes sought.
		Alternative, potential directions raised by these views are considered in light of		
		Kinds of changes envisioned.		
		Ultimate effect of these changes on problems in life arena, on people in arena, and on overall community.		
		Feasibility of avenues.		
2. Prepare Action Worksheets.	1 to 2 months (again, a culminating activity some of which is done concurrently with past activities)	*Action Worksheet outline—areas to be covered* Problem situation within the life arena. Brief statement of situation to be dealt with in a given Action Worksheet.	Guided by the working stance, choose to explore certain problem situations as they relate to potential change efforts. Begin preparation of Action Worksheets as you start looking at the life arena in depth.	

113

Sequential Steps	Approx. Time	Pertinent Information	Procedural Considerations	Conclusions and Decisions
		Nature and extent of problem situation. Non local and local evidence as to the nature and extent of problem or need.	Incorporate information obtained in study of the life arena generally and locally into Action Worksheets.	
		Existing services dealing with the problem. Descriptive statement of services.	Information in Action Worksheets will be both subjective and objective.	
		Change aids. Aids of the following nature which could be brought to bear in changing a problem situation:	Action Worksheets are not exhaustive or mutually exclusive. Many problem situations overlap or can be explored at different levels.	Begin narrowing range of possible target areas for change.
		Potential service resource. Who *could* be providing what type of service?		
		Program ideas. What are other communities doing?		
		Groups. What local and nonlocal groups or individuals could play a part in bringing about change?		

114

Sequential Steps	Approx. Time	Pertinent Information	Procedural Considerations	Conclusions and Decisions
		Laws.		
		Money.		
		Possible changes. What might be done, what is needed, and what is feasible?		
		Potential lines of activity. Alternative options for change. What could you do in bringing about these changes?		
3. Select target areas for change.	2 weeks	*Guidelines for Selection.* Analyze problem situations and possible target areas in terms of the following:	The decision regarding which target areas to pursue is accomplished via an informed, but still arbitrary, decision-making process. Decisions will be made by community professional and sponsoring body or another designated group.	
		Definition of the scope. How many target areas will be selected? This depends on number of community pro-		

115

Sequential Steps	Approx. Time	Pertinent Information	Procedural Considerations	Conclusions and Decisions
		fessionals employed, length of time of the effort, and number and kind of potential and feasible lines of activity which can be foreseen within any target area.	Potential target areas are not necessarily synomous with each problem situation as organized in the Action Work-sheets. A potential target area may cut across several problem situations or may be more narrowly defined and deal with only a small portion of one problem situation covered in the Action Work-sheets.	
		Need. Determine greatest need in terms of local services or programs to deal with the problem situation.	Procedures for selection:	
		Adaptability. Would people in the life arena and others necessarily involved in the change, adapt to the change?	Assess potential target areas using guidelines.	
		Numbers and significance. How many people in the life arena would benefit from change in proposed target area and how much would they benefit?	Group the potential target areas into closely related sets of target areas.	
			Assess the various groupings, using guidelines.	

Sequential Steps	Approx. Time	Pertinent Information	Procedural Considerations	Conclusions and Decisions
		Time input. Amount of time needed to bring about change.		Select target areas in which changes will be sought. This will direct as well as limit the involvement and actions.
		Flexibility of plans.		
		Viability of target areas. Viability of possible alliances.		
		Combining power. Could change in one target area affect change in others?		
		Feasibility. Time, money, manpower, information, and skills that could aid in change efforts.		
4. Select lines of activity.	continues	*Lines of activity emerge as you do the following:* Make probes regarding various change ideas in a target area.	Lines of activity are not necessarily selected all at the same time or immediately following the selection of target areas. Reach an agreement with the sponsoring body about the constraints and flexibility of decision-making in pursuing or dropping a line of activity.	

117

Sequential Steps	Approx. Time	Pertinent Information	Procedural Considerations	Conclusions and Decisions
		Receive feedback as to community groups' response to these probes.	When opportunistic situations arise that call for immediate decisions, you need the necessary autonomy to make those decisions independently.	Select lines of activity.
		Weigh the potential for pursuing a given line of activity (consider factors set down in guidelines for selection of target areas).		
C. Use methods, guidelines, and tactics for action.	continues	*Overall methods:*	*External Guidelines for Action: Negotiation and Communication Made Strategic*	
		Negotiation:		
		Obtain a negotiating alliance for a change idea.	Control the input of information and bargaining powers you bring to negotiation.	
		Negotiate the change idea into a change plan, including commitments on part of all parties involved.	Evaluate all situations for the existence of a possible opportunity to realize desired payoffs so that you can act quickly, yet knowledgeably, if the opportunity does materialize.	
		Carry out commitments made.		
		Communication:		

118

Sequential Steps	Approx. Time	Pertinent Information	Procedural Considerations	Conclusions and Decisions
		Form individual communication networks around lines of activity by receiving, sorting, and disseminating information.	Anticipate the existence of a chance to realize some change ideas or plans and then plan so that you time your actions in a way that takes full advantage of any ensuing opportunity.	
		Disseminate information by controlling who receives the information; by giving pertinent information (often short-circuiting it) only when some future action may result; and by strategically planning and managing the manner in which information is communicated.	Present the content of a communication in a style that is useful and at an appropriate level of specificity for the receiver.	
		Negotiation and Communication Tactics	Try to reach those people who either have the power to negotiate or to act on information or who are receptive to the information and may persuade others in power to act positively.	
		Probe. Investigate, search, explore, ask questions.	Attempt to disseminate information in a manner that keeps the information or a potential negotiation alive and working.	

Sequential Steps	Approx. Time	Pertinent Information	Procedural Considerations	Conclusions and Decisions
		Plant seeds. Plant an idea, suggestion, or information with the hope that it will sprout or grow.	Use negotiation or communication tactics as indicated.	
			Internal Guidelines for Action: Feedback, Evaluation, and Correction	
		Bargain. Reach a settlement on an issue or action by arriving at terms viewed as mutually agreeable or advantageous.	Focus on payoffs and outcome. Keep to the forefront of attention what has been done, where you are, and where you are headed in fulfilling the desired payoffs and realizing the change plan.	
		Stimulate. Provide a stimulus designated to motivate a person or group to react in a way you see as favorable.	Safeguard time. Keep track of time to ensure its wise allocation and careful use.	
		Consult. Engage in problem finding or solving wherein specialized help is given around a particular area.	Keep available and use important information. Communications and negotiations require keeping track of incoming and outgoing information for strategic use and	

120

Sequential Steps	Approx. Time	Pertinent Information	Procedural Considerations	Conclusions and Decisions
		Confront. Present information to others in a way that calls for a definite reaction on their part.	control, including the terms of each negotiation.	
		Ameliorate conflict. Act upon a situation in such a way as to diminish tensions resulting from differing points of view.	Receive feedback from actions. Information indicating the result of your actions must be returned so that you can make the necessary adjustments and corrections in plans and actions toward fulfilling a change plan.	
		Support and reassure. Provide supportive measures such as morale-building in a manner which would enable forward movement.	Make rational decisions. Base decisions on various considerations (time, desired outcome), alternatives (alternate change ideas, courses of action, activities or tactics), and consequences of alternatives.	
		Inform. Give factual information without personal opinion or point of view.		
		Advise. Give information which includes an opinion or point of view.	Be accountable. Report your activities in a manner which permits others (lay boards,	

Sequential Steps	Approx. Time	Pertinent Information	Procedural Considerations	Conclusions and Decisions
		Flexible Role of Community Professional	executive directors, sanctioning bodies, others in field) to be readily apprised of operations in any or all lines of activity.	
		Depending on situation, community professional may take on role of advocate, enabler, change agent, broker, and so forth.		
			Community professional avoids become an integral part of formal or informal structures that require system maintenance or that inhibit him from taking action on his own.	
		He works on behalf of, rather than at direction of, any group (except for relationship with sponsoring body).		
D. Use internal procedures for action: feedback, evaluation, and correction.	continues	*Forms*	Complete Forecast Sheets prior to an action period, immediately following completion of the Review and Appraisal Sheets for the past action period. Entries deal with plans for future action period. Records include decisions and plan; time span being forecasted; date when activities will again be re-	Decisions are made as to future actions, payoffs which will be sought, time investments which will be made, lines of activity which will be added, altered, or discontinued.
		Forecast Sheets. A depository, by major lines of activity, for forecasting future time investments, proposed actions, and anticipated payoffs or outcomes.		

122

Sequential Steps	Approx. Time	Pertinent Information	Procedural Considerations	Conclusions and Decisions
			viewed; amount of time being allocated; and payoffs desired and the predicted outcome.	
		Journal Sheets. A depository for recording all relevant information chronologically by major lines of activity.	Include all information you may wish to retrieve at a later time, keep a time record of, or review for evaluation. Make entries as the activities take place during the course of the following: telephone calls, conferences and meetings, think sessions, compiling a list of "things to do," or writing a letter or memo.	
		Review and Appraisal Sheets. A depository, by major lines of activity, for summarizing past events in light of prior forecast; appraising where line of activity is heading; appraising nature and degree of commitments; appraising	Complete Review and Appraisal Sheets at the end of one month action period. Records include summary of previous action period activity; time span being reviewed; amount of time allocated, time actually spent,	

Sequential Steps	Approx. Time	Pertinent Information	Procedural Considerations	Conclusions and Decisions
		and comparing payoffs, and courses of action.	and the difference between these two; payoffs forecasted and the actual outcome.	
		Time Tally Sheets. A depository for recording time spent and forecasted for all lines of activity. It indicates time available for further allocations to existing or new activities, or whether time is being overallocated.	Complete Time Tally Sheets at the time of each review and forecast. Records include a listing of the time which had been forecasted in prior action period for each line of activity; time actually spent for each during that period; difference between time forecasted and time spent; and the time forecasted for the next action period.	
			Keep an Action File, organized by target areas and lines of activity. House all incoming and outgoing materials that are part of the action effort, such as memorandums, news releases, or incoming correspondence.	

124

TRIAL OF THE BILATERAL PLANNING AND ACTION APPROACH: AN OVERVIEW

FROM PROBLEMS OF AGING TO ACTION ON AGING

Sequential Steps	Approx. Time	Procedural Considerations	Pertinent Information Obtained	Conclusions and Decisions
Obtained information necessary for action.				
Reviewed literature concerning aging.	1 month	Research assistants were used to review some of the literature.	Identified characteristics of the elderly.	
		Completed an annotated bibliography.	Identified numerous problems facing the elderly, such as income, health, lack of employment opportunities, lack of social role, isolation, and housing.	
		Prepared a paper summarizing problem conditions facing the elderly.	It was found that many problems facing elderly are not inherent in aging per se but rather stem from society's attitude toward and treatment of the elderly.	
		Began summarizing information into Action Worksheets.		

Sequential Steps	Approx. Time	Procedural Considerations	Pertinent Information Obtained	Conclusions and Decisions
		Began developing Planning File and Aging (life arena) Information File.	The previously held theory of the natural withdrawal of elderly from active participation in community life was found to be under fire and greatly disputed. Emphasis now on group consciousness and finding needed and meaningful opportunities for older persons to contribute to community life.	
Conducted a community change review.	2-4 weeks	Interviewed approximately 15 people from various segments of the community.	Segmented, diverse community, really 4 or 5 separate communities.	Could operate rather flexibly for change among various areas of community.
		Analyzed interviews and wrote a report.	No clear pattern to changes, usually occur slowly.	Could not anticipate major changes in attitude or policies in ⸮ brief time period.
		Began developing Community Agency and Organization File.	Segmented health and welfare network. Social action groups arising primarily in response to a crisis.	
			Diverse leadership, no core group identified.	

126

Sequential Steps	Approx. Time	Procedural Considerations	Pertinent Information Obtained	Conclusions and Decisions
Took a preliminary look at services being provided to older persons.	2 weeks	Contacts and calls to agencies and organizations were very informal. Information was compiled and attached to community review report.	Economic base is nonindustrial, primarily university-oriented. General knowledge of the kind of services available to older persons.	
Conducted a one-month study of social provisions for the elderly (October, 1968).	3 months	Study was directed and carried out by project research staff in communication with community professionals. Asked that services keep a one-month record of how much of what type of social provisions were given to how	Principal services provided were money and institutional care. Most community services were not utilized by older persons nearly as much as they were used by other age groups. There was a strong volunteer system of help, but this was primarily in institutional care of aging.	Lack of choice for independent living. Elderly not completely able to care for all aspects of their lives had little choice other than institutional care or living. Enough information was now available to arrive at a working stance.

127

Sequential Steps	Approx. Time	Procedural Considerations	Pertinent Information Obtained	Conclusions and Decisions
		many persons 60+. Social provisions are services, care, and income subsidized by taxes or voluntary contributions for which any elderly community resident may be eligible.	There were very few social provisions aimed at supporting independent living or a sense of independence.	
		Study was used for indicating need and for evaluating the approach, so was carried out in two additional counties for comparison purposes.		
		Resulting information for Champaign County was incorporated into Action Work-sheets as appropriate.		
Translated information into action.		The choice of a working stance was reached through numerous dialogues between the community professionals and the advisory group (project members).	High value in society placed on productivity, particularly economic, and the consequent isolation of people not actively participating in this. Also, many false stereotypes held regarding older people.	The working stance selected was that the overall change efforts will be directed toward the provision of services which would allow older persons to
Selected a working stance				

128

Sequential Steps	Approx. Time	Procedural Considerations	Pertinent Information Obtained	Conclusions and Decisions
		The attitudes reflected in the information obtained to date were considered in terms of the following: Kinds of changes envisioned. Given the attitudes held by society about productivity and pushing aside the unproductive, what changes are suggested. How would these changes affect the elderly and also the community? What avenues could be used in pursuing the changes, and how realistic were these avenues?	The reflection of attitudes found in the literature review and local study of elderly played an important part in selection of a working stance. The community professional's and advisory group's view was that although the elderly have many things in common, they also represent a cross-section of community life styles, values, and hopes, and thus should have a range of choices about such things as retirement, how independently they want to live, and how they want to participate in community life. It was also felt that because of the tradition of being pushed aside, older persons also needed	remain as independent as possible for as long as possible. It will be directed toward providing older people in Champaign County a range of choice in life styles along an independence-dependence continuum.

129

Sequential Steps	Approx. Time	Procedural Considerations	Pertinent Information Obtained	Conclusions and Decisions
			specialized services which would encourage them to make choices and use the available services to support such choices.	
Obtained information on possible change aids.	Process continues.	Placed name on appropriate mailing lists and subscribed to periodicals and magazines. Filed materials in Aging Information File.	Current concerns and needs.	
		Subscribed to major local papers. Clipped information potentially relevant to change efforts on behalf of elderly. Began developing Newspaper Clippings File.	Current programs and services being attempted. Legislative measures passed or being considered. What was happening locally, relevant to elderly. Local change aids: events, people, groups, money, conditions, etc.	
		Prepared Community Agency and Organization File identifying potential parties for negotiations, and persons or groups who might be in-		

130

Sequential Steps	Approx. Time	Procedural Considerations	Pertinent Information Obtained	Conclusions and Decisions
		volved in bringing about change.		
		Incorporated into the Action Worksheets information relevant to the problem areas they covered.		
		Used materials strategically.		
Prepared Action Worksheets.	1 month	Synthesized information obtained in previous steps, with orientation of working stance, into 11 separate Action Worksheets, each dealing with problem conditions or a set of closely related problem conditions.	Following areas were covered: economic, several aspects of health and home help, overall use of services, housing, role loss, transportation.	Analysis and synthesis of all information in order to select target areas.
		Numerous contacts and probes were made as necessary to obtain information on areas suggested in the outline for Action Worksheets.		
		Writing for materials on various subjects pertaining to		

131

Sequential Steps	Approx. Time	Procedural Considerations	Pertinent Information Obtained	Conclusions and Decisions
		elderly was started when total effort first began and continued throughout project.		
Selected target areas for change.	2 weeks	Assessed alternate target areas, using guidelines presented in the text. Grouped them into sets of target areas that were closely interrelated. Submitted the Action Work-sheets along with alternate sets of target areas to the advisory group. Based on these materials, the advisory group participated by each drawing up several potential target areas and potential lines of activity within these target areas. Based on these potential target areas, three target areas were submitted to the advisory group for approval.	Some of the potential sets of target areas considered were as follows: Role opportunities: employment, volunteer opportunities, recreation. Basic problems: employment, housing, health. Health: paramedical health services, home help, delivery of health services. Utilization of services: information and referral, demand for services (social action and group identity by elderly), and transportation.	Selected three interrelated target areas: 1. Employment. 2. Home-Health-Help. 3. Utilization of services.

Sequential Steps	Approx. Time	Procedural Considerations	Pertinent Information Obtained	Conclusions and Decisions

Selected and carried out several lines of activity.	9 months	Not all lines of activity were begun at one time. Throughout, lines were being added, dropped, or changed.
		
		Methods of communications and negotiations were actively used.
		
		Journal Sheets were completed daily as events took place.
		
		Monthly, each line of activity was assessed and plans for the next month were made through preparation of the Review and Appraisal Sheets, Forecast Sheets, and Time Tally Sheets. This took about 2 days each month, depending on number of lines in operation at the time.
			Information about aging, problems, services, change resources or helps, and community change was actively used throughout action period.	Pursued following lines of activity for each target area:
				1. Employment
				  a. Public Employment Service
				  b. Senior Talent Employment Pool (S.T.E.P.)
				  c. Community—general
				2. Home-Health-Help
				  a. Grocery delivery service
				  b. "Sitters for aging"
				  c. Medical social services

133

Sequential Steps	Approx. Time	Procedural Considerations	Pertinent Information Obtained	Conclusions and Decisions
		The above completed sheets were distributed to the advisory committee prior to meeting with them. They raised questions, made criticisms, and presented suggestions. As the community professionals felt necessary, advisors helped make decisions concerning which alternative lines of activity to pursue. However, the community professionals were directly responsible for making decisions to pursue each line. Continued to keep files current and developed Action File.		d. Motivate health network to action e. Community—general 3. Utilization of services a. Information, referral, and personal services program b. Transportation c. Senior citizens groups in rural areas d. Community—general

134

Sequential Steps	Time Approx.	Procedural Considerations	Pertinent Information Obtained	Conclusions and Decisions
Evaluated action Conducted a second one - month study of social provisions for the elderly (October, 1969).	2 months	Conducted same study as had been done before in Champaign County and two comparison counties. Some services that had no relation to the action efforts were dropped from the second study.		Positive change had taken place in areas relating to the target areas, although significance of the impact of the change effort could not be determined immediately upon completion of these efforts.

135

Appendix II

A SUGGESTED APPROACH:
A SOCIAL PROVISIONS STUDY

What are citizens getting in services, income, and care from health and welfare services? The community professional needs to know about the present distribution of social provisions before he attempts to initiate any change in that distribution.

"Social provisions" are services, care, and income subsidized by taxes or voluntary contributions for which any community resident from the selected life arena may be eligible. Social provisions, therefore, exclude services that are purchased by the user, and services provided by family and friends or by organizations for their own members.

A study of social provisions has two major objectives:

1. To find out how much income, care, and service the people in the life arena are actually receiving.
2. To identify actual community priorities in distribution of provisions to the people in the life arena and to spotlight major gaps in the provisions.

COMPREHENSIVE COVERAGE OF SURVEY

Fulfillment of this last objective requires the survey to be comprehensive. However, this does not mean that the survey needs to include every agency in the community. It does mean that the sample comprehensively represents services being provided.

The sample must be taken both from full-time, intramural care facilities, such as hospitals, and from extramural outpatient programs, such as community mental-health centers and county departments of public aid. All major organizations from the area

136

of community health, mental health, social welfare service, and recreation should be represented. Eliminate those organizations that do not apply to the people in the selected life arena. The sample should represent a range of auspices, both public and voluntary. Include out-of-county institutions, such as state mental hospitals, Veteran's Administration facilities, or other services to the life arena, for a comprehensive picture.

QUANTITATIVE DATA ON PROVISIONS

Finding out how much income, care, and service the people in the selected life arena are actually receiving requires you to collect quantitative data on provisions.

Examine actual social provisions to clients in three ways:

1. Headcount of clients.
2. Total cost of programs.
3. Hours of service and days of patient care.

Headcount of Clients

Counting the people in the life arena is one straightforward way of observing the service pattern. For most purposes, it does not matter whether the same head is counted twice (a duplicated count) during the time period selected for study. If an unduplicated count of clients is desired, however, it is necessary to obtain the names of persons.

Other characteristics of clients may be of special interest, e.g. age, sex, race, marital status, or religion. Gathering this information complicates the data collection process and extends the time necessary for data analysis.

Dollar Value of Provisions

A headcount of clients tells how many receive any provisions. But many citizens may receive very little. Therefore, it is also useful to learn how much is being given in money, services, and care.

One good measure of how much is being provided is the estimated dollar value of services and days of care, in addition to estimated total direct-money payments to clients during a sample month. Approximate the dollar value of agency contacts with clients by dividing the headcount of clients into the total agency salaries for the personnel who provide direct service.

Energies Expended on Behalf of Client Group

Obtain additional information on the question of how much agencies provide by counting the number of hours that staff spend in direct service to clients. Ask agency personnel to maintain survey records for an entire month. A less ambitious method to obtain similar results would be to ask for a three or four day, representative time study during a typical week. Agency administrators are able to define a typical week satisfactorily.

PROCEDURES FOR CARRYING OUT A SOCIAL PROVISIONS STUDY

Before beginning a social provisions study, you need to know something about the dimensions of the existing service structure, the number of clients being served, the auspices and location of major service providers, and any idiosyncracies or special problems in the local service organization that may affect the types of services chosen for study. Given this information, you then are prepared to make decisions more easily regarding sample size, variables to be included or excluded for study, and community characteristics requiring special attention in data analysis.

It may be helpful to categorize agencies and programs in the community along the following lines:

1. Intramural care (24-hour basis).
   a. General-care hospitals.
   b. Extended-care facilities.
   c. Psychiatric hospitals.
   d. Residential and custodial facilities.
   e. Educational and rehabilitation facilities.
   f. Correctional institutions.

2. Extramural services.
   a. Employment counseling and job retraining.
   b. Outpatient mental health and social welfare services.
   c. Income program interpretation.
   d. Outpatient medical and health information services.
   e. Recreation.

f. Education (elementary school, secondary school, university adult extramural).

3. Income maintenance.
   a. Direct payment programs.
   b. In-kind payments.

Programs or agencies also may be categorized by auspices.

1. Public programs.
   a. Federal.
   b. State.
   c. County.
   d. District.
   e. Municipal.

2. Private programs.
   a. Private, nonprofit.
   b. Voluntary, noncorporate.
   c. Proprietary.

Community Service Reconnoiter

The community reconnoiter can be undertaken in a number of ways, but there are four routes that may prove particularly helpful.

1. Obtain a list of formal agencies in the community from the local welfare directory, chamber of commerce, local planning bodies, and the telephone directory. Use the categories previously suggested to organize the list.

2. Make a spot check by telephone of current charitable services by fraternal and religious organizations that exist outside the formal health and welfare network.

3. Obtain copies of any recent community studies, including the current Census Reports and an annual United Way report, if available. Use this information to help ascertain such things as the population range and socioeconomic level of your community. Compare the census information to the amount of United Way support and the number of agencies funded.

4. Subscribe to your local newspaper; comb it daily to identify new action groups, issues in community policy-making, and sources of influence. The newspaper provides clues to newly developed services.

Selection of Study Sample

Using the outline of agencies and programs which you have developed during your reconnoiter, contact these organizations by letter. Ask for estimates of total case load or patient load per month, average number of clients from the selected life arena, average monthly direct payments to clients, and cost-of-service data, if available. Group the agencies by type of service, set up a tally sheet and record the data received.

When complete, the tally sheet gives you a rough picture of total provision activity and magnitude of cost. The content of agency responses indicates the programs with little or no relevance for the selected life arena, the agencies that pose more difficulties in providing data, and the agencies with the greatest responsibility for various types of service.

One effective way of reducing the sample size, while still obtaining a good overall picture, is to establish a minimum average patient or client load as a criterion for inclusion of agencies in the survey. For example, you may choose to drop any agency serving less than fifty persons on an average monthly basis. The effect of this rule may be to limit the survey to those agencies that serve eighty percent of the selected life arena population.

However, since the sample needs to represent a comprehensive picture of provisions, another method of reducing sample size may be to confine the study to the major providers in each category of service, i.e. those offering about seventy-five percent of the total community service to the selected life arena in any given category of services.

Some other factors to be taken into consideration in sample selection follow:

1. Study only those programs offering ongoing, rather than intermittent, service. Services depending on spontaneous good will or erratic funding are not likely to have much real impact on the client population.

2. Give preference to services which are county-wide in scope with the exception of recreational programs. The object in a social provisions survey is to learn which services are accessible to any community resident, given his need. Neighborhood programs usually have a fairly limited potential clientele, and again, often exercise an insubstantial effect on the total provisions scene.

3. Study services with some potential for providing help to the client population. For example, if aging persons were the selected life arena, the local Muscular Dystrophy Association could be dropped from the sample simply because the elderly are unlikely to have this disease.

Data Collection

Data collection must be undertaken with tact and consideration for the agencies involved, not only because agency cooperation hinges on your attitude and approach but also because the life arena population may be affected indirectly. If agencies are positively engaged in the study, interest and effort on behalf of the life arena population may increase also. Furthermore, you lay the groundwork for future cooperation by these agencies in follow-up studies, planning activities, or community action. Good relations, not mechanics, must be foremost at this point.

The data-collection phase of the social provisions study begins with the final determination of the variables to be studied and the programs to be included. A research form to be completed by workers in the programs being studied is prepared then.

The next steps are as follows:

1. Write a statement of survey purposes, which clearly identifies the auspices for the project. This statement is used in contacting agencies; most will request a written explanation.

2. Obtain examples of other social provisions studies for distribution to agencies who want to know how data will be used.*

*Taber, Merlin, Itzin, Frank, and Turner, William: *A Comprehensive Analysis of Health and Welfare Services for Older Persons in One Community.* Iowa City, Iowa: Institute of Gerontology, State University of Iowa, September, 1963.

3. Organize a notebook for the work activity of any assistants to be employed. The notebook should include a full explanation of the study; instructions for interviewing; names, addresses, and telephone numbers of organizations in the sample; and a form on which to indicate the status of ongoing contacts with involved agencies. Detailed notes should be kept on comments by administrators, suspected problems, observations of factors affecting the validity of data from individual organizations, and data about client population obtained through interviews.

4. Develop a filing system for completed research schedules.

Initiate contacts with agencies in the sample, preferably by personal interview. Give sample research forms to the agency administrator well in advance of actual data collection.

Once you have the cooperation of organizations, remain available for questions. During the time that agency workers are recording their activities, it is worthwhile to check with as many agencies as possible to make certain that the administrator has not forgotten, that forms have not been lost, or that the agreement has not in some way broken down.

Expect about fifty percent of the agencies to return their completed research forms without prompting and two or three follow-up calls. It probably is best to visit the agencies personally at the end of data collection and to pick up the forms yourself.

Data Analysis

Data analysis begins during the data collection phase, as completed research forms start returning. Tabulation sheets with clearly defined categories for analysis must be set up as soon as any concrete data becomes available. You need to know at a glance which agencies returned incomplete forms or, equally crucial, where accumulated data is not yielding the desired information about community provisions.

Work out the final interpretation of findings with great room for creativity and flexibility. Three perspectives for data analysis are suggested below, but other alternatives, of course, abound.

1. Use your hunches. During the data collection process, you

begin to get some intuitions about possible relations between variables and overall study outcomes. Write down these "guesses" for more formal analysis.

2. Use your target areas. If there are special problems which you have in mind as target areas for action, then develop categories for analysis which reflect volume and distribution of provisions in these target areas.

3. Do not forget the total community. However you narrow your focus, do not ignore an analysis of the total context in which problems are taking place. Set up baseline data about the overall functioning of the community health and welfare network, in which size of provisions is the principle concern.

Data Feedback

Aim data feedback, the final phase of your study, at three audiences:

1. The general public, via news media.
2. The total community health and welfare network.
3. Any social-action group with which you are working or plan to work.

Each audience requires a somewhat different format in data presentation. Take care that confidentiality is not breached. Prepare individual agency reports by type of service, or make a summary of the total community. The extent of these reports depends on time, financial resources, and action plans. It should be stressed that this data feedback is an integral aspect of data collection, but unfortunately it is the feature of community-service studies most often ignored.

ILLUSTRATIVE EXAMPLE OF AN ACTION WORKSHEET: EMPLOYMENT FOR OLDER WORKERS

I. Problem or Need: Lack of employment opportunities for aging persons.

II. Nature and Extent of the Problem Situation.
   A. Nonlocal.

   1. See mimeographed paper of 7/24/68 by N. Rempe, Staff Associate, summarizing problems of aging, "Aging: Nature of the Problem." Folder by title in Aging Information File.

   2. Earnings are still the major source of income for older persons. The 1963 Social Security Administration Survey of the Aged indicated in the breakdown of the aggregate money income of persons 65 and over, that more than 30 per cent was from earnings. See President's Council on Aging, *A Time of Progress for Older Americans,* 1965-1967 Report on the President's Council on Aging (Washington, D.C.: U. S. Government Printing Office, 1968), p. 11.

   3. In 1965, the United States Department of Labor found that 17 per cent of the population over 65 were in the labor force, either working or actively seeking work. This includes 24 per cent of the older men and 10 per cent of the older women. However, the 1960 statistics show that only one out of 6 men and one out of 25 women, age 65 and over, were year-around, full-time workers. The majority of older people who work have part-time jobs or are employed for only part of the

year and are employed in low-pay work. However, the 17 per cent over 65 in the labor force comprise only 4 per cent of the total United States labor force. See Gerontological Society, Projects Division, "Fact Sheet on Aging," (St. Louis: Gerontological Society, 1966, mimeographed).

4. Retirement benefits of Social Security reveal the lack of freedom an aging person has regarding retirement income. Social Security provides for an optional early retirement from 62 to 64 years of age but at reduced benefits. For example, the man who retires at age 62, with a wife the same age, receives a maximum monthly benefit of about $150, as compared with a benefit of $190 if he retired when he and his wife were age 65. The early retirement option with its reduced benefits, often used by those who cannot find jobs, reduces the retirement income of persons whose income would be extremely low even without such reduction. See Juanita M. Kreps, "Employment Policy and Income Maintenance for the Aged." In John C. McKinney and Frank T. deVyver (Eds.): *Aging and Social Policy* (New York: Appleton-Century-Crofts, 1966), p. 148.

5. Persons receiving Social Security cannot retain the full benefits if their yearly earnings exceed 1,680 dollars. On earnings up to 2,880 dollars, one dollar of benefits is subtracted for every two dollars earned. If earnings are over 2,880 dollars, one dollar is subtracted for every dollar earned. Because of the red tape and potential holdup of needed Social Security checks resulting from earnings of over 1,680 dollars, many older persons are reluctant to become employed in jobs which they may not be physically or emotionally able to continue.

6. In addition to the earning restrictions placed on older persons by Social Security, other pension plans also have restrictions.

7. See Bernard Kutner, *et al.: Five Hundred Over Sixty,* (New York: Russell Sage Foundation, 1956). Kutner, in his study of 500 people over age 60, reported the following:

    a. The largest decline in morale or adjustment of those over 60 occurs in the 65-69 age group.

    b. To play a role in the productive economy, when coupled with good health, is predictive of a favorable adjustment.

    c. Of all the values involved in adjustment to retirement, the feeling of being useful and wanted is paramount.

    d. Many older people require activities in retirement that will be substantial functional substitutes for the responsibilities of gainful employment, family rearing, and homemaking.

    e. Within each activity level group, the employed have higher morale than the other employment status groups.

8. Older persons face the loss of worker or breadwinner role.

    a. See Ethel Shanas, *et al.: Old People in Three Industrial Societies* (New York: Atherton Press, 1968). In the study reported, 33 per cent of the respondents who had been retired three years or less said that they wanted work. Of those respondents retired over three years, 19 per cent wanted to work.

    b. The role of worker in our society is seen as primary and is highly prized. Compensating structural alternatives, however, are not yet built into our industrial society. See Irving Rosow, *Social Integration of the Aged* (New York: The Free Press, 1967).

9. The United States Bureau of the Census indicates that in 1966 some 20 per cent of the 58 million households

in the United States were headed by persons aged 65 or over. Between 1960 and 1966, the number of older households increased faster (14%) than did younger households (9%). In households of 65 and over, female heads are increasing one and one-half times as fast as households with under-65 female heads. Among those household heads over 65, less than half have a male head of the household. This suggests the need for placing some emphasis upon training, retraining, and rehabilitation for employment among older women.

10. Also see summaries of or notes on the following publications, Aging Information File.

   a. Wayne Kirschner, "The Attitudes of Special Groups Toward the Employment of Older Persons" (*Journal of Gerontology*, vol. 12, 1957, pp. 216-220).
   b. Juanita Kreps (Ed.): *Employment, Income and Retirement Problems of the Aged* (Durham, N. C.: Duke University Press, 1963).
   c. Harold Orback and Clark Tibbits (Eds.), *Aging and the Economy* (Ann Arbor: University of Michigan Press, 1963).
   d. Erdman Palmore, "Work Experience and Earnings of the Aged in 1962: Findings of the 1963 Survey of the Aged" (*Social Security Bulletin*, vol. 27, June, 1964, pp. 3-14).
   e. *Increasing Employment Opportunities for the Elderly*. Hearings before the Subcommitte on Employment and Retirement Incomes of the Special Committee on Aging, U. S. Senate, 88th Congress, 1963. Statement by Donald P. Kent, pp. 28-30.
   f. Harold Sheppard, "Unemployment Experiences of Older Workers" (*Geriatrics*, vol. 15 (1960) pp. 430-433).
   g. Jacob Tuckman and Irving Lorge, "The Attitudes of the Aged Toward Older Workers" (*Journal of Gerontology*, vol. 7, 1952, pp. 559-564).
   h. Jacob Tuckman and Irving Lorge, "Attitudes To-

ward Older Workers" (*Journal of Applied Psychology,* vol. 36, 1952, pp. 149-153).

i. U. S. Department of Labor, *The Older American Worker: Age Discrimination in Employment,* (Washington, D.C.: Department of Labor, 1965).

j. Leroy Johnson and George B. Strother, "Job Expectations and Retirement Planning" (*Journal of Gerontology,* Vol. 17, No. 4, October, 1962, pp. 418-423).

k. Juanita Kreps and Ralph Laws, *Automation and the Older Worker.* An annotated bibliography prepared for the Committee on Employment of the National Council on the Aging (New York: National Council on Aging, 1963).

B. Local (see Planning File).

1. Returns from the social provisions study conducted in Champaign County during October, 1968, revealed that only 21 people age 60 and over (.02 of 1% of total population over 60) were served during October, 1968, by the public and voluntary employment services in Champaign County. A total of 1,182 persons were served by these agencies. This indicated a very low utilization of employment services by older people. For further details, see "Existing Services Dealing With the Problem."

2. The employment services in Champaign County are primarily geared toward permanent, full or part-time employment in the business and industrial community. The private job placement and temporary job placement services deal almost exclusively in secretarial and heavy industrial areas.

3. The social provisions study revealed that one of the primary sources of all services for the elderly is found in the voluntary sector of the community. Consequently, this sector might have the greatest potential for developing employment services most appropriate to elderly persons.

4. The greatest manpower need and shortage in Champaign County seems to be in the service area. Members of the community, including older persons, do not have access to part-time, flexible, temporary help, particularly in the home and in small businesses. Because this is a university community, the maintenance businesses are understandably more interested in the larger apartment house contracts than in a one-hour job for an older person.

5. There are no preretirement or retirement planning programs in the county.

6. Only 480 persons age 65 and over were receiving Old Age Assistance in October, 1968. This is less than 15% of the total population over age 65.

III. Existing Services Dealing with the Problem.

A. Public.

1. Public Employment Service.

A job counseling and placement service. Some job development is done with large employers, primarily industry.

The social provisions study in October, 1968, revealed that during that month, they served a total of 900 persons. Of these, only 11 were age 60 and over. They were not very eager to participate in this study and had to be convinced by higher officials.

The state organization has developed several special employment services, one being for elderly persons. However, due to the size of the local office, no special personnel are assigned to this service and, consequently, it receives little attention. Of its special services, most attention is given to the youth program.

The reputation of this service in the community is rather shaky. Its leadership has been criticized by other agencies seeking some cooperative effort.

2. Vocational Rehabilitation Service.

This is a rehabilitative and retraining service. Its rehabilitation is aimed not only at making people employable at permanent, full-time jobs, but also at rehabilitating persons for part-time, occasional employment, such as baby sitting.

This local office does not have facilities for retraining. They make referrals to the Vocational Rehabilitation Training Centers or to other agencies.

The social provisions study revealed that during October, 1968, a total of 98 persons were served. Only 10 were age 60 and over. The services provided to these older persons were primarily financial paramedical services.

B. Private, voluntary.
1. Community League.

One service provided by this agency is job counseling and placement, being involved specifically in breaking down racial barriers to employment. The emphasis is on youth.

During October, 1968, they served 90 persons, none of which were over 60 and report that they rarely do. In terms of priority of needs, they feel they cannot give emphasis to elderly persons.

2. Job Training Center.

This is a rather new job counseling, job training, and job finding service for disadvantaged persons. Many aspects of this program are still being developed.

Although they served no one 60 or over during October, 1968, they indicated a desire to do so in the future.

3. Rehabilitation Center.

This is a rehabilitation and training center for physically, socially, and mentaly handicapped persons. Although its purpose is that of evaluation and training for job placement within the community or rehabilitation center, its emphasis appears to be oriented toward the center through contracting piecework employment from local businesses.

Of the 27 persons served during October, 1968, none were age 60 and over.

Agencies which make referrals to this service feel that some reorganization and redirection is needed. Rehabilitation and training or retraining needs to be oriented more toward placement in the community. As it now stands, it is almost as though all the clients become permanently employed at the Center or become permanent clients.

C. Private employment services.

    1. Service XYZ.

        This is primarily a temporary help service. The agency contracts for jobs which are then filled by their own employees, such as secretarial help for industry, loading trucks, etc.

        The newspapers have given a great deal of publicity to their summer youthpower program. This is a job placement service for youth. Need to find out more about this.

    2. Employment Service P, temporary service.

    3. White Glove Services, temporary help service.

    4. Placement Service W, both temporary help and permanent job placement service.

    5. Personnel Service A, permanent placement service.

    6. B and B Personnel Consultants, permanent placement.

IV. Change Aids.

A. Potential service resources.

    1. Expansion of already existing services (see above) to include more older persons.

    2. Major community employers. See employment folder in Action File.

        a. University Personnel Office.

        b. County schools and school districts. Potential for

employment in such areas as teacher aids and training in these areas.

c. Industries, O, T, and X, primarily factory work.

d. Hospitals: Y, E, M, and L.

e. Air Force base.

3. Potential training, retraining, and rehabilitation services.

   a. University.

      1) Vocational-Technical Education.

      2) Home Economics Department. Miss D, in that department is developing a curriculum for persons working with groups of older persons (Sheltered Care, Nursing Homes). Potential for including older persons in training curriculum.

      3) University Homemaker Extension Service. They are developing a nutrition aid program with training program to start soon.

   b. Junior College. They are developing many vocational-technical training programs.

   c. Commercial College. Rather limited potential.

   d. Adult Education Program Q. Following contacts for the social provisions study, the head of this program expressed interest in broadening their program to include more older persons. He went so far as to eliminate all tuition fees for older persons. Potential may exist for training in areas relevant to older workers. However, this would be a completely new idea from the program as it now exists.

   e. Adult Education Program R. They have a Licensed Practical Nurse training program. Have trained very few persons over 60. Not adverse to idea if older person is healthy.

   f. Public Health Department. Could develop (or contract to develop) training in auxiliary health fields, such as home-health aids.

   g. Public and voluntary welfare service agencies.

Could develop training and employment programs to fill manpower needs.

4. Other potential services.
    a. Community Action Program. None of the many federal programs dealing with employment operate locally. However, present status of the program is so shaky that provision of any service in this area is doubtful.
    b. Voluntary organizations, such as local National Council of Women's Group J, women's clubs, professional clubs. See program ideas.
    c. Institutional and outpatient treatment facilities for children, such as Kamp's Children's Home or the Regional Treatment Center. Perhaps they could use the government-subsidized "Foster Grandparent" program.
    d. Business throughout the county.

5. Retirement planning services.
    a. Businesses. Some of the locally-centered national businesses, such as Industry T, have well-developed retirement planning services at their central facilities. For T's program in Chicago, see folder on retirement planning, Aging Information File.
    b. Local chambers of commerce. Since area has a preponderance of smaller businesses, could develop one central program.
    c. Social service agencies, such as Social Service Agency P or Mental Health Agency C. Could also develop a central program.
    d. Federation of Labor.
    e. Churches or civic groups. In Newton, Kansas, a community mental health facility, in cooperation with several churches, has developed retirement planning and retirement preparation programs.
    f. Senior citizens and retired persons' groups. See Community Agency and Organization File. Only group which exists locally is a retired teacher's

group. However, they really do not have, at present, a retirement planning service.

B. Program ideas.
  1. The following are Model Community Action Programs, Office of Economic Opportunity. Mimeographed materials or pamphlets on each, prepared by the National Council on the Aging, are found in the employment folder in the Aging Information File.

    a. A home maintenance and repair program for the older poor.
    b. Project TLC (Tender Loving Care), program to employ older people as aides to work with very young children. The report details the project which calls for recruiting, training, and employing older people in a variety of institutions which serve children.
    c. Project SWAP (Senior Worker Action Program), program to promote recruitment, counseling, and job placement of older workers. The report is an excellent resource providing much background information on the nature and extent of the employment problem for older persons and detailing development of job opportunities and new employment possibilities for senior citizens.

  2. The Foster Grandparent Program is a program employing men and women over age 60 with incomes below the poverty index. The program is administered by the Administration on Aging under contract with the Office of Economic Opportunity. See "The Foster Grandparent Program—A New Role for Senior Citizens" (*Public Aid in Illinois,* vol. 34, no. 9, September, 1967 pp. 2-8).

  3. An Employment Solicitation Project is a project of the National Council of Jewish Women, 1 W. 47th Street, New York City. See employment folder, Aging Information File, for mimeographed publication entitled

"Selling Experienced Manpower," which presents a detailed guide on the solicitation project. It also describes other types of services, such as vocational guidance and retraining programs and legislative activities. Also presented is an outline for a sample training course and a large bibliography on readings, films, and organizational resources.

4. The Good Neighbor Aide Program is a free, over 60 counseling, training, and job placement service offered by the Montgomery County, Maryland, Federation of Women's Clubs. They report a high success ratio. See employment folder, Aging Information File.

5. See *Proceedings of the National Conference on Manpower Training and the Older Worker.* Sponsored by the National Council on Aging and United States Departments of Labor and Health, Education, and Welfare, Washington, D.C., January 17-19, 1966. (On bookshelf, under "Employment.")

a. One workshop report. "New Fields of Employment and Vocational Training," identified many new possibilities for employment and training of older workers. Among those specifically mentioned for further exploration and definition on a national basis were occupations in the school lunch program, homemakers and nursing home aides, agro-business occupations, senior home repairers, keepers of public property legally impounded by civic authority, home health aids, and a wide variety of full and part-time job possibilities identified in connection with OEO activities.

b. Some of the work categories suggested in many of the discussions include handyman, gardener, companion, and service to social agencies, such as schools, hospitals, libraries, community chests, family services, and day care programs. The categories have developed from a felt need in the community, in addition to the special needs of many older persons, i.e. part-time employment and flexibility.

c. On pages 242-249, a speech is presented, outlining new programs for employment of aging persons developed under CAP (Community Action Program) sponsorship.

6. "In addition to the maintenance of program priorities for older poor persons, in 1966, the Office of Economic Opportunity created a special unit for programs for older persons in the community action program of OEO. Since July of 1966, Mr. Daniel Schulder has functioned as director of older persons' programs for CAP within the Office of Program Planning. As director of older persons' programs, Mr. Schulder has inaugurated a comprehensive review of CAP activities on behalf of older persons and has directed the development of program policies and guides designed to assure that all components of CAP as well as other programs of OEO (such as VISTA, Head Start, etc.) serve the needs of older persons either through employment opportunities or through the redirection of program services." See United States Senate, Special Committee on Aging, *Development in Aging, 1966,* 89th Congress, p. 26.

7. Service Core of Retired Executives (SCORE), operated by the Small Business Administration, is a program by which retired executives offer consultation to small businesses with fewer than 25 employees who could not otherwise afford consultants. See folder on employment, Aging Information File. Also see the following issues of *Aging:* June, 1963; April, 1964; October, 1967; and May, 1968.

8. See section under Funds.

9. See International Association of Machinists and Aerospace Workers, *Guide for Older Workers and Retired Members Programs* (Washington, D.C.: International

Association of Machinists and Aerospace Workers, no date). Employment folder, Aging Information File.

10. See John F. Kennedy Family Service Center, Inc., *Older Workers Training and Employment Program* (Charlestown, Mass.: John F. Kennedy Family Service Center, Inc., 1967). Bookshelf.

11. A demonstration project, Corps of Senior Citizens Teacher Aides, was conducted by the Dade County, Florida, Public Schools as Federal Project 9477 during the school year of 1967-68. "Data obtained from a number of instruments indicate that senior citizens are able to perform a wide variety of noninstructional tasks which support the teacher, the pupil, and the school itself in pursuit of educational objectives. Not only is the presence of the senior citizen in the school situation fully acceptable to the administration, staff and students involved, but the services he renders as a para-professional are enthusiastically received. For the senior citizen, employment as a teacher aide is personally appealing and financially worthwhile. More-over, such indirect benefits as enhanced self confidence, strengthened self esteem, and enlarged outlook which he often derives may provide humanistic values of even greater significance." See Dade County Board of Public Instruction, "Operation Seasoned Service, A Report of the Corps of Senior Citizens Teacher Aides," published by the Administration on Aging, United States Department of Health, Education, and Welfare as *Senior Citizens as Teacher Aides,* 1968. (Bookshelf.)

12. See *Final Report of "Project 60" An Experimental and Demonstration Program for Older Workers,* December 1964-April 1967, San Francisco, California (Washington, D.C.: United States Government Printing Office, 1968, 0-312-591). (Bookshelf.)

C. Groups.

1. State and regional offices of the Public Employment

Service. See discussion under local service, over which regional office has policy making powers.

2. State Labor Commission.

3. State Division of Administration on Aging. See Community Agency and Organization File. Resources for consultation and financial support for programs.

4. Chamber of Commerce. Could perhaps help us reach businesses or provide a forum for education, pressure, dissemination of information. Also have just started a club for their retired members. Need to explore this group—might be interested in SCORE.

5. Office of Economic Opportunity, national and regional offices. Could provide financial resources for bringing to this community many of their programs. First, need to explore local manpower needs for their programs.

6. See funding sources.

7. The Henderson Grain Elevator Company, a large new company in the area, has recently run a series of ads on a radio station to recruit employees. One of their selling points was "no forced retirement." It might be interesting to see how they arrived at this policy, what results the policy has had, and if they would be interested in making this information available to other employers in this area.

8. Mass media. See Community Agency and Organization File.

9. Social action or pressure groups: Women Voters Organization, Community Improvement Coordinating Council. This latter group is new, made up of several prominent, action-oriented businessmen. Seem to have more clout than any other action group. They have set up a citizens' complaints committee upon which their action efforts will be based. Complaints about employment opportunities and practices relating to older persons might spur some action.

D. Laws.

1. "Age Discrimination in Employment Act of 1967." Purpose of the act: to promote employment of older persons based on their ability rather than age; to prohibit arbitrary age discrimination in employment; to help employers and workers find ways of meeting problems arising from the impact of age on employment. It became Public Law 90-202 on 12/15/67 and covers employees and would-be-employees, ages 40-64.

2. Older Americans Act of 1965 (OAA). This act created the Administration on Aging and provides for Federal assistance to State Commissions on Aging.

3. Nelson Amendment to the Economic Opportunity Act. (find out more about.)

4. See "Funds."

E. Funds.

1. The Vocational Education Act of 1963 provides for a large-based Vocational-Technical Education Program primarily for public schools. The United States Office of Education makes grants to states on a 50-50 matching basis. The State Vocational Education Agency is the administrating agency. This program serves older people by supporting:

   a. Vocational education for older adults who need training or retraining to achieve stable employment or advancement.

   b. Special training for those older persons having academic or socioeconomic handicaps that prevent them from succeeding in the regular vocational programs.

   c. Technical training of personnel to serve in such capacities as a companion to an elderly person and nurse's aide.

   d. Construction of area vocational education facilities, which may be designed with special features for older people.

2. The Manpower Development and Training Act of 1962 and amendments of 1966, Public Law 89-15, provides for several training programs beneficial for older persons. They are administered jointly by the Office of Education of the Department of Labor and the Office of Education of the Department of Health, Education, and Welfare. They provide the following.

   a. Training for older workers (over age 45) who need employment. Increasing emphasis is being given to this group as a result of the "older worker" amendment of 1966. It requires, "where appropriate, a special program of testing, counseling, selection, and referral of persons 45 years of age or older for occupational training and further schooling designed to meet the special problems."

   b. Training for paraprofessionals, such as nurse's aides and occupational therapy aides, who will serve older people.

   c. Refresher training for unemployed persons, including professionals such as registered nurses, many of whom will be serving older people.

For further information see folder on federal and state funds, Aging Information File. Places to write are presented.

3. Title V of the OAA authorizes grants to support specialized training of persons employed in, or preparing for, employment in programs related to the broad purposes of the act. One of the stated priorities is to support "leadership training for members of state and community committees on aging and for older adults who wish to become active within their communities" and also "training for semiprofessional direction is library and recreation aides, aide in housing projects, homes for the aged, in institutions, in homemaking and meal services, and in a variety of other ways" (these persons could also be older persons). For details, see *Developments in Aging,* 1966.

4. Title IV of the OAA authorizes grants and contracts to develop new and better methods and facilities in meeting the needs of older people: grants made directly to, or through contract with, a public or nonprofit private agency, organization, or institution, and, in the case of a contract, with an individual. A pertinent kind of demonstration project currently being funded is training older persons to help reach other more isolated elderly with information, guidance, and personal service and to stimulate their interest in community and group affairs.

5. National Council of Senior Citizens, Inc., Washington, has 15-month $1,129,520 contract to provide 400 jobs at minimum of $1.60 per hr. and maximum of $3,000 per yr. as "Senior Aides" in public and nonprofit community agencies such as schools, hospitals, and nursing homes. Jobs will be provided in 10 cities yet to be selected but in target geographic areas, such as Model Cities. Contracts were made under the Manpower Development & Training Act and the Nelson Amendment to the Economic Opportunity Act. (See *Aging*, 4/68, p. 6.)

6. National Council on the Aging, New York City, has 15-month $1,096,111 contract to provide 400 jobs at $1,800 annually or minimum of $1.60 hourly for part-time work in community service programs. Work will include visiting and assisting handicapped older persons, providing follow-up for persons discharged from hospitals and rehabilitation centers and for Head Start and Job Corps enrollees. Workers will be recruited through the United States Employment Service for projects in Model Cities target areas. For unemployed or retired men and women over 55. Contracts were made under the MDTA and the Nelson Amendment to the EOA (see *Aging*, 4/68).

7. Senior Aide Employment Program: (National Council of Senior Citizens). NCSC has awarded funds to public

and nonprofit agencies for nine projects providing 360 jobs for people 55 years of age or older. Source of the funds is a 15-month $1,093,840 grant NCSC received from the United States Department of Labor in February, 1968. Under the program, part-time jobs, which have not been available because of lack of local funds, will be offered as senior aides in schools, libraries, hospitals, nursing homes, public health agencies, social welfare agencies, public recreation centers, and other community agencies. For details of programs funded, see *Aging,* Aug.-Sept., 1968, p. 21.

8. Training Grants of the Vocational Rehabilitation Administration provide financial assistance to increase the supply of qualified personnel for service, research, and teaching in fields related to the rehabilitation of individuals having physical, mental, or emotional disabilities. Although VRA does not regard aging as a disability per se, it recognizes that disabling conditions are more prevalent among older people than younger ones. For further information, contact Chief, Division of Training, Vocational Rehabilitation Administration, Department of Health, Education, and Welfare, Washington, D.C. 20201.

9. See The President's Committee on Employment of the Handicapped. *Employment Assistance for the Handicapped.* A Directory of Federal and State Programs to Help the Handicapped to Employment. (Washington, D.C.: United States Government Printing Office, 1967.) (On bookshelf, under employment.)

10. See Department of Business and Economic Development, *State of Illinois Catalog of Programs for Individual and Community Development.* A description of state programs to help individuals and communities meet their own goals for economic and social development, (Springfield, Illinois: Department of Business and Economic Deveopment, January, 1967). Bookshelf.

11. See the National Council on the Aging and the Office of Economic Opportunity, *Resources for the Aging: An Action Handbook* (New York: National Council on the Aging, February, 1967). (Bookshelf.)

V. Possible Changes.

A. Development of job resources for older people.

B. Creation of relevant job opportunities for aging persons, particularly for flexible, part-time employment.

C. Development of flexible retirement policies by employers.

D. Development of preretirement planning programs.

E. Retainment and hiring of more older workers by small businesses.

F. Provision of special counseling and placement services for older persons by established local employment agencies.

G. Development of pilot projects by volunteer community organizations for the elderly which might be outside the charge of public agencies (too costly or time consuming).

H. Development of services which would supplement and support the work of employment agencies and individual businesses, such as vocational counseling, training, and retirement counseling.

I. Establishment of auxiliary services for those capable of handling only limited employment, such as earning-learning shops, sheltered workshops, or home craft shops.

J. Development of training or retraining programs for the aging either within the business or service community.

VI. Potential Lines of Activity: Alternative Options for Change.

A. Approach all public and private employment agencies in town with results of social provisions study, information on needs, and suggestions as to how they can better include older persons in their service. (Primarily relates to possible change A, B, E.)

B. Stimulate a community group to launch a public information campaign directed primarily at employers of the community—much like the "Hire the Handicapped" campaign, but locally based with local figures—the goal is to create more flexible hiring policies by indicating the need, the myth of stereotypes, the "experience power," etc., of older persons. This could be done through the Chamber of Commerce or the Jaycee's, with sponsorship of both city governments, etc. A large employer recently had commercials on a radio station which included a statement to the fact that in their hiring practices, age was not a consideration and they had no enforced retirement policy—this could be an opportunistic situation (depending on their present relationship with other community employers), could use them as an example. (Primarily relates to possible changes C, D, E.)

C. Approach the local office of the private employment agency, Service XYZ, about the possibility of setting up and advertising a "Senior Citizen Register" for part-time jobs such as (for men) lawn work, odd jobs about the home, surveys, janitorial services, etc.; (for women) office work if proficient in typing and shorthand, telephone surveys, general clerical, people sitters for persons who might be incapacitated, baby sitters, etc. Service XYZ expressed an interest in cooperating to make "Action on Aging" a success in their letter to us dated 11/4/68 (on file). There is a need in the community for such temporary and/or part-time services and this kind of work often fits in well with the older person's need to earn limited income but not too much to jeopardize their Social Security benefits. Also, at times, the physical inability to work full-time, but capacity to work part-time, can be a factor. (Primarily applies to possible changes A, B, F, H, I.)

D. Approach a community-service group, with a potential volunteer corps, who could be motivated to action regarding employment problems of older workers. At the national level, the National Council of Women's Group J has done a great deal in the area of the older worker. Their booklet has sample programs of several varieties and very explicit guidelines for direction. Perhaps the local affiliate might be approached. Find out more about this. If this is not a possibility, then another service-oriented community group could be contacted. (Primarily related to possible changes A, B, G, H, I.)

E. When (and if) time permits, approach other change resources in an open-ended way to feel out the interest level of specific individuals, etc., and then attempt to capitalize on it in whatever manner might appropriately suggest itself. (Relates generally to all possible changes.)

F. Approach educational institutions about expanding their adult education programs to include specifically older persons, especially in the area of vocational technical education such as retraining for more sedentary skills. (Primarily relates to possible changes B, I, J.)

G. Approach some public or private agency (perhaps Public Employment Service) to establish a registry specificially helping with employment. Two major components would be a retired person's employment registry and development of a service which actively seeks out employment opportunities or engages in development of jobs for older persons. (Primarily relates to possible changes A, B, F.)

Appendix IV

ILLUSTRATIVE SAMPLE PRESENTING THE DEVELOPMENT OF ONE LINE OF ACTIVITY: THE SENIOR TALENT EMPLOYMENT POOL

The Senior Talent Employment Pool (S.T.E.P.) serves as an employment pool for aging persons. It provides older persons the opportunity for flexible, part-time employment, as well as serving as a clearinghouse through which homeowners, housewives, clubs, service organizations, and small businesses can utilize the skills of these older people for various jobs. S.T.E.P. is sponsored and operated by Women's Club K.

The story of S.T.E.P. is told to illustrate more graphically the Bilateral Approach in action. Some of the information and ideas set down in the Action Worksheet on Employment (Appendix III) set the stage for the presentation of the major activities of the community professionals in fulfilling the S.T.E.P. change plan. In this appendix, samples of the Review and Appraisal Sheets and Forecast Sheets are used to illustrate the activity, feedback, evaluation, and planning.

CREATING CHANGE: THE STORY OF S.T.E.P.

In the initial change efforts as community professional, lines of communication were cultivated and developed by informing the community of Action on Aging's existence. Personal contacts were made and memorandums sent to the mass media, agencies, and groups relevant to aging, and particularly to those change aids that were important to the target areas, such as employment.

Service XYZ, a private, temporary job placement service, sent a letter of interest in response to this communication. Based on this letter and knowing that the manager had a personal interest in the elderly, the decision was made to probe and cultivate further this line of communication.

166

The meeting with Mrs. X from Service XYZ began as a probe, but quickly turned into a seed-planting session when the clearinghouse idea was favorably received by Mrs. X. During the meeting, full use was made of prior knowledge and information gained in the meeting: Mrs. X's personal interest in the elderly, her experience with an employment program for youth and the close relationship between that program and the clearinghouse idea, Mrs. X's membership in Women's Club K, Women's Club K's national project on geriatrics and the local chapter's interest in a project. Because the response to the clearinghouse idea was so well received, the meeting actually became the first bargaining session toward negotiating the idea into a definite plan.

Prior planning had primarily involved the possibility of interesting Service XYZ in an employment clearinghouse program for the elderly. However, in this meeting, the change idea and the potential alliance for negotiating the idea were redirected toward a voluntary organization and away from an existing employment service. (See Figs. 16 and 17).

Development of the plan continued, often using tactics of bargaining, stimulating, support, and reassurance with Mrs. X as she prepared to present the idea to a Women's Club K meeting.

Focus on the broader target area of employment during this period also continued. The community professionals did not want to put all of their eggs in one basket, particularly since Women's Club K had not made a definite commitment. Probes and a slightly different employment service were presented to the Public Employment Service, although any positive response from them was doubtful. However, when they agreed at least to negotiate about it, it was immediately anticipated that there might be some problem with Mrs. X because of an historically keen competition between this public and private agency. The community professionals began to clarify and specify the difference in their own minds. The difference was, however, primarily determined by what the two groups were willing to negotiate. Women's Club K was interested only in temporary employment, using those registered for many different short-term jobs, whereas the Public Employment Service wanted to be involved primarily in permanent employment.

FIGURE 16

REVIEW AND APPRAISAL SHEET: EMPLOYMENT–GENERAL

ACTION ON AGING
Champaign County, Illinois

Date: 2/18/69

Target Area: Employment

Line of Activity: Employment–General

Summary: Notes and Findings

Time Span: 1/16/69–2/15/69
Time Spent: 10 hours
Time Allocated: 15 hours
Difference: $(+)$
$(-)$ 5 hours

1. Met with Manager of Service XYZ. We found out it is strictly a profit-making business with emphasis on clerical, industrial, and business; little room to move into the area of employment in home services; prices they charge for services in home would often be prohibitive to older persons as well as other home-owners.

a. Presented our idea of an employment clearinghouse for older persons, focusing on jobs around the home.

They operated a special program for youth last summer as a community service–supervised and provided facilities for employment clearinghouse for youth. Was a nonprofit com-munity service effort. Feel they can't take on another one for older persons.

b. However, Mrs. X is very interested in the idea and has given thought to how older persons might be able to help each other in various homemaking-home maintenance tasks.

Payoffs Forecasted–Actual Payoffs

1. Locate one agency or organization who would be sufficiently interested to begin at least some type of negotiations (tentative agreement) = good potential for one—Women's Club K.

2. One definite line of activity would emerge (yes) = no, but still hopeful.

c. As we put together the pieces as to how the service might work, we suggested Women's Club K of which she is a member. National project is gerontology. Might be interested. Said they were in need of a project. She agreed to present employment idea to them.

2. Probes were made in employment in area of home-health-help. It looks as though, for now at least, the public health service (Medicare Home-Health Agency) will not be contacted as a potential agency to provide home-health-help services, principally because Social Service Agency P has received several negative responses (as have several other agencies in the community) from them with regard to certifying for Medicare, the already-trained homemakers as home health-aids.

169

Review & Appraisal Sheet Number: 18

FIGURE 17

FORECAST SHEET: EMPLOYMENT—GENERAL

ACTION ON AGING
Champaign County, Illinois

Date: 2/18/69

Target Area: Employment

Line of Activity: Employment—General

Summary Notes on Decisions and Plans

1. Wait to see if Mrs. X presents idea to Women's Club K.

2. Continue probes regarding possibility of employing older persons in area of home-health-help.

3. Tentatively plan to contact other voluntary groups and other existing employment services, particularly the Public Employment Service, and perhaps the local affiliate of the National Council of Women's Group J, if there is one. Also bring up employment need and ideas of services opportunistically with all appropriate contacts.

Time Span: 2/16/69–3/15/69
New Review Date: 3/15/69
Time Allocated: 20 hours

Payoffs Forecasted

1. Locate one agency or organization who would be sufficiently interested to begin at least some type of negotiations: yes.

2. One definite line of activity will emerge: yes.

4. In approach to the Public Employment Service, go to them with the idea (G) in Action Worksheet on Employment under Potential Lines of Activity: Alternative Options for Change— plan for employment registry and job-finding and job-develop- ment service. This is a slightly different approach than we used with Service XYZ. Our meeting with them was generally unpro- ductive until we brought up a specific plan or idea. Also, use approach "what would it take for you to provide such a service" rather than "would you provide such a service?" We are not too optimistic at present time about their doing anything because (a) had to use "powers from above" to get them to participate in study of socially provided services, (b) have heard numerous complaints about their services, (c) have heard that other com- munity groups have had difficulty in working with the director.

171

Other voluntary groups were contacted (probings, seed planting, and stimulating). These were seen as possible new sources for negotiation around an employment clearinghouse idea should Women's Club K decline.

In order to obtain the necessary feedback for assessing progress, correcting actions, determining the payoffs desired, and organizing the change idea for different directions which were emerging, the record-keeping system was divided into four different lines. (See Figs. 18 and 19.)

Women's Club K indicated, through Mrs. X, that they were at least willing to negotiate the idea. The community professionals continued bargaining with her (and she with them) and began drawing up the terms of the negotiation for both parties. For example, Mrs. X said that Club K members would have to operate the service out of their homes via telephone and that they would need help with any finances necessary, since their fund-raising benefit had to be cancelled.

The community professionals kept track of what they had committed themselves to in helping Club K start the service: getting "skills" survey to older persons and related recruitment publicity, initial publicity for the service once it was established, and consultative assistance. Aspects of the negotiation and change ideas which would have to be worked out were also noted: funding for the service (telephone and other supplies), how clearinghouse lists would be kept up to date by all volunteers, role and tasks of coordinator (amount of time that would be involved). With each bargaining session, the employment clearinghouse idea was developing into a more concrete plan. These tentative plans and the terms of the negotiation were drawn up in a memo to be presented to the Women's Club K membership.

Plans were also continued (but less actively) for an alternative group to approach if Club K failed to make a definite commitment.

The definite commitment which Women's Club K made rested on the community professionals' fulfillment of the initial term of the negotiations, namely, recruitment of the first group of senior citizens. With this commitment a major change step had been fulfilled. The next major change step, recruiting enough older

FIGURE 18

REVIEW AND APPRAISAL SHEET: EMPLOYMENT–GENERAL

ACTION ON AGING   Date: 3/16/69
Champaign County, Illinois

Target Area: Employment   Line of Activity: Employment–General

Summary: Notes and Findings   Time Span: 2/16/69–3/15/69
                                                 Time Spent: 27 hours
                                                 Time Allocated: 20 hours
                                                 Difference: (+) 7 hours
                                                                (−)

1. Met with director and assistant from Public Employment Service
   (PES). Presented brief explanation of need and then our idea.   Payoffs Forecasted–Actual Payoffs
   Results were that they could have a registry for older applicants
   without disrupting internal operations greatly (could have brief   1. Locate one agency or organization who would be
   listing to refer to more complete file of applicants). Recognized   sufficiently interested to begin at least some type
   need for accompanying job development but couldn't provide   of negotiations (yes) = yes, two groups–PES and
   paid manpower for this. We presented possibility of using volun-   Mrs. X re: Women's Club K.
   teer manpower. They presented concern about agency's policy
   of confidentiality. This was solved when we suggested codes   2. One definite line of activity would emerge (yes)
   could be substituted for names. We agreed to present them with   = yes, about four different lines, only two with
   a more concrete plan based on our conversation. Results were   definite possibilities.
   more hopeful than anticipated although we question how much
   effort they will really expend other than giving a title to what
   they say they already do. We need to see if we can find a
   volunteer(s) who would be interested.

173

2. Met with Mrs. X in order to clarify what ideas she should present to Women's Club K. We again shared our ideas and hers (because of her experience in this area, she has many excellent ideas). Agreed that although total program initially should be geared toward homes and homeowners (maintenance, baby-sitting, etc.) rather than businesses, the first step would be getting a list of older persons who would like to be registered with a clearinghouse, and then seeing what their skills were. She is sold on idea and thinks she can sell Women's Club K.

3. Mrs. X knew about our contact with PES and her reaction was negative. She said it was because of the uncooperativeness of PES. However, we speculate she might be concerned about PES stealing the thunder from Women's Club K. We will have to clarify difference between services for both groups.

4. Initially, we presented two similar-type services to both Women's Club K and PES, anticipating that probably one of them wouldn't work out. However, both have potential and we need to clarify differences so each group doesn't see it as a issue of two groups providing the same service. The major difference we see is that the PES service would be geared toward finding permanent, part-time or full-time jobs for older persons. The clearinghouse idea with Women's Club K would be geared toward temporary, flexible, part-time employment.

5. Did some seed-planting with other voluntary groups in the community in an effort to stimulate them toward initiating some

174

type of employment service for older persons. We presented need rather than a specific idea or plan. Wrote a letter to Women's Group T (closest local organization to National Council of Women's Group J) and spoke to a community-action committee of a local church seeking a project on behalf of elderly. If Women's Club K negotiations don't develop, we will have our feet in the door to present clearinghouse plan to them. We are inclined to think this idea would best fit in a volunteer organization at this time because (a) existing employment agencies place emphasis on permanent-type employment with business and industrial firms and (b) the temporary employment agencies place emphasis on heavy industrial and maintenance jobs. The latter group also has prohibitive cost rates for families and older persons wanting to use their service.

6. Have had several informal contacts with Mr. S of Social Service Agency P regarding home-health-help. He indicated that he was planning to find a coordinator for their Homemaker Service and that perhaps they could think about expanding or taking on some other functions at a later date.

7. Our complete lack of knowledge about the employment community or more specifically, all existing enterprises and employers, has led us to consider making a limited study of the employment and retirement policies, number of persons employed, manpower needs and skills which could be filled by an older person, problems encountered in employing older persons, etc. Although we don't have a specific change plan, we feel

175

such a study could help us in making more knowledgeable decisions about lines of activities and change plans. It might also be plugged into idea being negotiated with PES. Also, the study might have possibilities for some type of educational campaign directed at relevant concerns of employers. A sample of different types of employers could be included in study by using the categories established for the United Way campaign.

8. Since we are actively pursuing several change ideas in employment, the following will tentatively be made into separate lines of activity:

   a. Employment registry—PES.

   b. Clearinghouse—Women's Club or other voluntary group.

   c. Employment community.

   d. Employment general—will include employment in home health-help since we don't have definite activities.

Forecast Sheets will be divided into these areas.

FIGURE 19

FORECAST SHEET: EMPLOYMENT—CLEARINGHOUSE

Date: 3/17/69

ACTION ON AGING
Champaign County, Illinois

Target Area: Employment

Line of Activity: Employment—Clearinghouse

Time Span: 3/16/69–4/15/69
New Review Date: 4/15/69
Time Allocated: 15 hours

Summary Notes on Decisions and Plans

1. Continue contact with Mrs. X of Women's Club K. If Club K indicates any interest, we will draw up a memo spelling out plan and how we could help. This will allow their group to consider the plan more knowledgeably.

2. If efforts with Club K result in response of only guarded interest, more actively pursue groups such as Women's Group T or Community Action Committee of Church C.

3. Deciding amount of time to allocate is difficult—so much depends on response from Women's Club K.

Payoffs Forecasted:

1. Mrs. X will present idea to Women's Club K: yes.

2. Will receive a tentative agreement from members of Club K that they are interested in negotiating idea: yes.

3. "Official" expressions of interest from group(s) other than Club K: no.

Forecast Sheet Number: 42

persons, became the thrust of the community professionals' activities. In addition, a commitment was made to help them raise initial funds to get the service started. (See Figs. 20 and 21.)

The commitment of recruiting enough older persons to start an employment pool was carried out through widespread use of, and cooperation by, the mass media in addition to broad distribution of skills checklist form and covering letter. The skills checklist form included the following list of skills and talents:

Please Check:

MEN

Carpentry: Rough_____Finish_____
Cabinetmaking_____
Electrician_____
Plumber_____
Painter: Outside_____Inside_____
General Home Repairs_____
Heavy Cleaning: Window washing
_____Wall washing_____Floor
care_____
Bartending_____
Gardening_____Landscaping_____
Chauffeur_____
Barber_____
Odd Jobs_____
Other (name)_____

WOMEN

Baby-sitting_____
Sewing: Mending_____
Tailoring_____Alterations_____
Cooking: Plain_____Fancy_____
Baking_____
Hostess Helper_____
Laundry: Washing_____ Ironing_____
Light Housework_____
Clerical: Typing_____ Filing_____
Hand Addressing_____
Other (name)_____
Beauty Care: Hair Dresser_____
Manicurer_____
Other (name)_____

MEN OR WOMEN

People-sitters (sitting with older
people)_____
Musicians: Teaching_____
Performing_____
Upholstering_____

Bookkeeping_____
Tutoring_____
Nursing Aides_____
Animal sitting (for vaca-
tioners)_____

For approximately a month, the returns were noted, relating the number received to the time and effort spent. This analysis revealed that results were definitely much less than anticipated for the amount of effort expended. Unless the payoff was greater during the next month, without additional time and effort input on the part of the community professionals, serious evaluation would need to be made regarding whether to continue with this

FIGURE 20

REVIEW AND APPRAISAL SHEET: EMPLOYMENT–CLEARINGHOUSE

ACTION ON AGING   Date: 5/15/69
Champaign County, Illinois

Target Area: Employment   Line of Activity: Clearinghouse–S.T.E.P.

Summary: Notes and Findings   Time Span: 4/18/69-5/15/69
                                    Time Spent: 14 hours
                                    Time Allocated: 20 hours
                                    Difference: (+)
                                                 (−) 6 hours

1. Received a definite "go-ahead" from Women's Club K. They
   will run clearinghouse for part-time employment of older persons   Payoffs Forecasted–Actual Payoffs
   provided we can recruit enough older persons to start the ser-
   vice. Will be called "S.T.E.P." (Senior Talent Employment   1. Definite commitment from Women's Club K or
   Pool). Until enough persons are recruited, Club K doesn't want   another group to operate "clearinghouse" employ-
   to be involved publicly. Mrs. X has found two women who are   ment service (yes) = yes, Women's Club K, pro-
   willing to coordinate the service (Mrs. S and Mrs. D) and   vided we fulfill certain commitments of help.
   several other members who will volunteer to man the telephone.

2. Devised a skills checklist form and cover letter to be mailed to
   older persons and taken to groups of senior citizens and related
   groups jointly with Mrs. X. We will do the recruitment through
   use of the skill form to be completed by those interested, and
   then we will turn this information over to Club K. Mrs. X will
   train volunteers. The service will operate through a telephone
   answering service.

3. Women's Club K prefers own answering service but needs $450-$500 for 1-year period. An alternative is sharing TELE-CARE answering service.

4. Need to now work on:
   a. Get mailings out, answer telephone inquiries, and receive and hold returns.
   b. Find a funding source.
   c. Devise mechanics for running service productively and efficiently.

5. There is some resistance by Club K toward PES program (at least by Mrs. X). We've had to be very tactful and should continue to do so.

FIGURE 21

FORECAST SHEET: S.T.E.P.

ACTION ON AGING
Champaign County, Illinois

Target Area: Employment

Line of Activity: S.T.E.P.

Date: 5/15/69

Time Span: 5/15/69–6/15/69
New Review Date: 6/15/69
Time Allocated: 30 hours

Review & Appraisal Sheet Number: 65

Summary Notes on Decisions and Plans

1. Continue to carry out following commitments in helping service get organized:

Payoffs Forecasted

1. Number of returns of skill forms from older persons: 25.

2. Procure a definite funding source: locate cne contributor.

a. Get skills checklist forms and cover letters out to older persons. We are using only our name at this point. Write publicity releases directed at recruitment. Also do a mass mailing.

b. If returns sufficient for Women's Club K to start service, assist with publicity of new service under name of Club K. Number of returns necessary has not been established. Depends on skills indicated on returns.

c. Find a funding source. Follow through with prior contacts with United Way Director. If United Way effort fails, other groups for potential funding are Service Club R, E Club, military and fraternal organizations. Will contact as needed or as opportunity arises.

d. Continue to offer administrative assistance in developing service.

2. We don't anticipate the service actually starting or operating during this month.

3. Continue to use support and reassurance relative to Mrs. X's resistance to PES program. Protect her interest.

Forecast Sheets Number: 67

line of activity. This possibility was anticipated and other alternatives explored.

However, during the following month, the number actually recruited exceeded the number which had been forecasted, indicating progress toward achieving the desired payoff of recruiting enough older persons to start S.T.E.P. Initial feedback from communication efforts regarding recruitment revealed interest not only on the part of older persons, but also from potential users of S.T.E.P.

Based on evidence that the initial commitment to Women's Club K for recruitment would be fulfilled, assistance could now be given with fund-raising, with the mechanics and details of the service, and any consultative assistance they requested.

With the aid of a couple of opportunistic situations, the change step of obtaining monies for beginning S.T.E.P. was substantially completed. Although no definite money figure was designated in the bargaining, the community professionals had agreed to try to raise enough for the first six months of operation. Certain contacts which had been initiated for fund-raising purposes were, of course, continued.

In addition, the commitment in the area of initial publicity for the service was fulfilled with the preparation of a S.T.E.P. brochure. Screening applicants for the pool, recruiting volunteers to staff the service, and setting up the mechanics of the service were commitments Women's Club K actively assumed.

It had been pointed out to Club K that except for a brief period of consultation, they would be on their own once the service began. This fact was stressed as more members of the group became actively involved. (See Figs. 22 and 23.)

Women's Club K began its major commitment as the service actually started.

In addition to some continued effort with funding and publicity, the community professionals' attention turned to the final payoff desired, that of operating a service which people would use. A slow start had been anticipated, just as recruitment had started very slowly, but the actual outcome went far above what had been forecasted.

A great deal of consultative assistance and reassurance was not

FIGURE 22

REVIEW AND APPRAISAL SHEET–S.T.E.P.

ACTION ON AGING   Date: 8/27/69
Champaign County, Illinois

Line of Activity: Senior Talent Employment Pool

Target Area: Employment

Time Span: 7/15/69-8/15/69
Time Spent: 55 hours
Time Allocated: 40 hours
Difference: (+) 15 hours
                   (−)

Summary: Notes and Findings

1. Commitment made to help with initial fund-raising is substantially fulfilled.

   a. Made use of an opportunistic situation to raise funds for
      S.T.E.P.–organized, with help of Mrs. S from Women's Club
      K, the participation of Club K members and their friends
      in a telephone research project. Raised approximately $180.

   b. Received a lead that the Missions Commission of Broadmoor
      Methodist Church might be interested in contributing finan-
      cially to S.T.E.P. Wrote a formal request to them on behalf
      of Club K for funds. Received a reply that they would con-
      tribute $50.00.

2. The two coordinators of S.T.E.P., Mrs. S and Mrs. D, have
   become actively involved. We have met and talked often with
   Mrs. X and them about actual mechanics of setting up and coordinating S.T.E.P.

Payoffs Forecasted–Actual Payoffs

1. Number of returns of skill forms from older persons (35 total) = 43.

2. Number of men recruited (10) = 8.

3. Procurement of definite funding sources for 1st
   year (good potential for "yes") = procured $230
   out of approximately $450 needed or about 50%.

4. Completion of mechanics of operating service–
   forms and procedures (yes) = yes, about complete.

a. Revised initial record-keeping forms and system which Mrs. X drew up.

b. They've recruited enough Club K volunteers to start service and have made the major decision as to how volunteers will operate.

c. Agreed with Club K's plan to start S.T.E.P. on September 2, 1969.

d. We revised and made up large quantities of S.T.E.P. brochures for community distribution. Did some distributing.

e. Drew up list of women's clubs and other organizations to whom brochures could be given. Women's Club K agreed to assume responsibility for future distributing. We'll help if time permits.

f. Mrs. X agreed to take the responsibility for publicity once service started.

g. Contracted for business telephone and answering service in name of Club K.

3. Continued, through news media, to recruit actively more men in order to have a better male-female ratio.

4. With the above activities, we have virtually completed our commitments, except for more help in initial publicity and following through on any responses to past fund-raising overtures.

5. Number of Club K volunteers to participate in operation of service (10) = 2 coordinators and 9 women so far.

Review & Appraisal Sheet Number: 138

FIGURE 23

FORECAST SHEET: S.T.E.P.

ACTION ON AGING
Champaign County, Illinois

Date: 8/27/69

Target Area: Employment

Line of Activity: Senior Talent Employment Pool

Time Span: 8/16/69-9/15/69
New Review Date: 9/15/69
Time Allocated: 25 hours

Summary Notes on Decisions and Plans

1. Write initial news releases, arrange for pictures, etc.

2. Evaluate procedures and record-keeping system with Women's Club K during this time period, revising as necessary.

3. Help in distribution of brochures if Club K becomes overwhelmed.

4. Continue to help find funding sources to meet 1st year's budget of $450.00.

5. Continue radio and other mass media publicity for recruitment purposes and advertising the service to the community.

Payoffs Forecasted

1. Number of calls for 9/2-9/15 for S.T.E.P.: 5.

2. Number of new persons on registry: 3.

3. Amount of funding procured: $50.

4. Inches of publicity and minutes of radio and TV coverage: 15 inches and 10 minutes.

Forecast Sheet Number: 139

185

necessary once the service started. Many problems had been ironed out through the experienced aid of Mrs. X and the community professionals' help in carefully setting up the mechanics of the service.

With the fulfillment of all change steps, the community professionals phased out active involvement with Club K and S.T.E.P. Although periodic consultative assistance has been given upon request by Club K, it is felt that they, with the help of other community groups, can make any necessary adjustments or changes in the service.

GLOSSARY OF TERMS AND CONCEPTS

Action. *See* Action File; Action Worksheets; Bilateral Planning and Action Approach.

Action File. A file of memorandums, letters, news media releases, speeches, and local incoming correspondence that are part of the effort for change. It also contains information on local change aids.

Action Worksheets. Written summary acounts of the information gathered about a problem situation or area for development in the selected life arena. These are also a record of the community professional's analysis of what and who could bring about change and how this might be accomplished best.

Activity. *See* Line of activity.

Advise. To give information that includes the community professional's opinion or point of view, such as favoring one possible action over another.

Agency. *See* Community Agency and Organization File.

Aids. *See* Change aids.

Ameliorate conflict. To act in such a way as to diminish tensions that result from differing points of view. The community professional may or may not be implicated directly in the conflict.

Appraisal. *See* Review and Appraisal Sheet.

Approach. *See* Bilateral Planning and Action Approach.

Area. *See* Target areas for change.

Arena. *See* Life arena.

Bargain. To reach a settlement on an issue or action by arriving at terms that are viewed as mutually agreeable or advantageous. All parties involved can expect to give up something in order to get something else.

Bilateral. To indicate and emphasize that the community professional, on his own initiative, energetically reaches out to one or more selected groups or individuals in an effort to enter into communication or negotiation around a change idea.

Bilateral Planning and Action Approach. An approach to obtain desired change in a specified arena of community life. The community professional acts to bring about change in selected target areas through the establishment of time-limited negotiating alliances and through the strategic use of communication, leading to the fulfillment of a change plan.

Change. The new and different about people, situations, or things.

Change aids. Any existing or potential resource that could effect some change in the existing condition(s) of a particular situation, person or persons.

Change idea. An idea about the way to alleviate or prevent a particular problem or to provide opportunities for development. Feasibility of the idea or the steps involved has not necessarily been established.

Change plan. A change idea that has strong potential for being realized in a feasible, concrete outcome or goal. Essentially, it is an idea for which some of the actual steps have been defined and, at times, carried out.

Change steps. The specific, incremental, short-term, component actions that are necessary to achieve the realization of the change plan.

Change aids, change ideas, change plans, change steps. All concepts that denote changes which relate to correcting recognized problems, lacks, and deficiencies, or making use of unused opportunities that are not dependent upon unmet needs for their justification. Examples of the former are ideas to correct underutilization of services, restore equity or redress wrongs, alter educational outcomes such as the number of children reading below grade level at the time of graduation. Examples of unused opportunities are creation of new services, importation of new program resources, economic growth and expansion of employment opportunities. Small-scale as well as large-scale innovations may be involved.

Clipping. *See* Newspaper Clipping File.

Communication. To receive, sort, and relay information, signals, or messages by such things as talk, writing, gestures, or silences. As a method of action, it is the careful management of information and messages by the community professional.

Community Agency and Organization File. A file containing the names, addresses, and brief pertinent information about groups and people in the community who can be viewed as existing or potential change aids.

Community professional. A professional who originates or advances change ideas selectively by (a) developing and using communication networks to short-circuit information and fill information gaps at an appropriately specific level and (b) negotiating these ideas into feasible change plans and helping to carry the negotiated plans to completion through discrete change steps.

Conflict. *See* Ameliorate conflict.

Confront. To present information to others in a way that calls for a definite reaction on their part. This implies that the community professional already knows the stance or prior action of the group and that his view is at variance with their views or policies, either stated or inherent. It serves to sharpen the issue; it points up the consequences to which the current course is leading or has led.

Consult. To engage in problem finding or problem solving through providing specialized help around a particular area.

Correction. *See* Feedback and correction.

Feedback and correction. A system of record-keeping where the results of activity that are necessary to make adjustments and corrections in plans are identified by the community professional. Information about these activities serves as a new platform from which to regulate future action.

File. *See* Action File; Community Agency and Organization File; Life Arena Information File; Newspaper Clipping File; Planning File.

Forecast Sheet. A form that is prepared for each line of activity and serves as the current plan of action (and referent for action) until the next periodic assessment. It includes space for listing future time allocations, proposed action, and anticipated payoffs and outcomes.

Groups. *See* Selected group.

Idea. *See* Change idea.

Individual. *See* Selected group or individuals.

Inform. To give factual information that does not reflect the community professional's personal opinion or point of view.

Journal Sheet. A form that is a chronological depository for recording all activities and outcomes by lines of activity. It includes decisions, actions, and results, in addition to preparation, thinking, and planning. It is useful for organizing day-by-day work, for ensuring continuity of effort, and for facilitating reflective thought.

Life arena. The sector of community life around which the directed change efforts take place. This includes both the specific population group on behalf of whom change is sought and the institutions that strongly influence the life style and opportunities for these people.

Life Arena Information File. A file that houses nonlocal information concerning the life arena. It includes information from the review of literature about specific areas that pertain to the arena.

Line of activity. A coherent set of change ideas or a plan that the community professional pursues within a target area. Lines of activity are interrelated and potentially convergent, but for the sake of clarity, planning, and accountability, each line is viewed separately.

Negotiation. A method of action in which the community professional enters into an alliance (with one or more parties) that involves coming to an agreement on the terms of a change plan and taking the steps necessary to fulfill the plan.

Negotiated change plan. The result of bargaining that is carried on between the community professional and the other party. It is an agreed-upon proposal to alter specific outcomes, plus an agreement on the actions, organizational changes, or allocations of resources that are regarded as necessary to bring about the change, e.g. establishment of an older worker's employment registry and a job development service.

Newspaper Clipping File. A file that houses and organizes selected local newspaper articles which are related to the life arena and the local community, and any other articles which indicate potential change aids.

Organization. *See* Community Agency and Organization File.

Payoff. One in a series of short-term change steps which marks progress toward realization of an intended change plan or idea.

Plan. *See* Change plan.

Planning. *See* Bilateral Planning and Action Approach; Planning File.

Planning File. A file that houses information directly related to change efforts in the community, such as informal or informal studies of the local life arena, the community review, Action Worksheets, and any materials evolving from the process of selecting target areas.

Plant seeds. A tactic whereby the community professional plants an idea, suggestion, or specific information with the hope that it will sprout and develop. He makes statements or requests that suggest a direction, a course of action, or a desired response.

Probe. To question. The community professional asks for a response that will put him in a better position to frame a subsequent request, to take a certain action, or to make a future decision. The intent of the probe may include opening up a dialogue or an avenue for communication, discovering the degree of readiness and receptivity to change ideas, determining the availability of unused or untapped opportunities, or ascertaining the nature of decision-making.

Professional. *See* Community professional.

Provisions. *See* Social provisions.

Reassure. *See* Support and reassure.

Review and Appraisal Sheet. A form that is designed to summarize and assess a month's work on each line of activity. It shows action taken, time invested, and payoffs achieved. It allows the community professional to appraise where the line of activity is heading, the nature and degree of commitments made, and payoffs and courses of action. It further provides a review and summarization of recent past events as they relate to past forecasts.

Selected group or individual. The other party to the negotiation or communication that is selected because of its vested interest, key position, control of resources, state of readiness, responsiveness, or other attributes which are relevant to the change idea.

Sheet. *See* Action Worksheet, Forecast Sheet, Journal Sheet, Review and Appraisal Sheet, Time Tally Sheet.

Social provisions. Services, care, and income that are subsidized by taxes or voluntary contributions for which any community resident from the selected life arena may be eligible. Social provisions, therefore, exclude services purchased by the user, services provided by family and friends, and services by organizations for their own members.

Stance. *See* Working stance.

Steps. *See* Change steps.

Suggest. *See* Plant seeds.

Support and reassure. To provide necessary supportive measures, such as morale building and praising, in a manner that will enable an individual or group to move forward in a direction which will further a change idea or plan.

Target areas. *See* Target areas for change.

Target areas for change. Concrete problem situations or particular areas for development in a given life arena around which the community professional focuses change efforts.

Time Tally Sheet. A form for recording time spent and forecasted for all lines of activity. It indicates time available for further allocation to existing or new activities or whether time is being over-alloted.

Working stance. A statement of the overall direction of the change effort. It guides decisions and actions and spells out the broad who, what, and how of the community professional's efforts. It defines what is desirable and indicates an avenue for moving in this direction.

BIBLIOGRAPHY
OVERVIEW

Biddle, William W.: *The Community Development Process.* New York: Holt, Rinehart and Winston, 1965.

Buckley, Walter: Society as a Complex Adaptive System. In Buckley, Walter (Ed.): *Modern Systems Research for the Behavioral Scientist.* Chicago: Aldine, 1968.

Dunham, Arthur: *The New Community Organization.* New York: Thomas Y. Crowell, 1970.

Dyckman, John A.: Social planning, social planners, and planned societies. *Journal of the American Institute of Planners,* 32:66-75, March, 1966.

Etzioni, Amitai: *Readings in Modern Organization.* Englewood Cliffs, N.J.: Prentice-Hall, 1969.

Etzioni, Amitai: *Studies in Social Change.* New York: Holt, Rinehart, and Winston, 1966.

Etzioni, Amitai and Etzioni, Eva. (Eds.): *Social Change: Sources, Patterns, and Consequences.* New York: Basic Books, 1964.

Frieden, Bernard and Morris, Robert: *Urban Planning and Social Policy,* New York: Basic Books, 1968.

Goodman, Leonard H. (Ed.): *Economic Progress and Social Welfare.* New York and London: Columbia University Press, 1966.

Gould, Julius and Kolb, William L. (Eds.): *A Dictionary of the Social Sciences.* New York: Free Press of Glencoe, 1964.

Greer, Scott, *et al.* (Eds.): *The New Urbanization.* New York: St. Martin's Press, 1968.

International Conference of Social Work: *Social Progress Through Social Planning.* Report of the United States Committee to the 12th International Conference of Social Work, Athens, Greece, September, 1964. New York: United States Committee of the International Conference of Social Work, 1964.

Kramer, Ralph M. and Specht, Harry (Eds.): *Readings in Community Organization Practice.* Englewood Cliffs, N.J.: Prentice-Hall, 1969.

Kravitz, Sanford: "Sources of Leadership Input for Social Welfare

Planning." Unpublished Ph.D. dissertation, Brandeis University, Waltham, Mass., 1963.

Lippitt, Ronald, Watson, Jeanne, and Westley, Bruce: *The Dynamics of Planned Change.* New York: Harcourt, Brace and World, 1958.

Marris, Peter and Rein, Martin: *Dilemmas of Social Reform: Poverty and Community Action in the United States.* New York: Atherton Press, 1967.

Meyerson, Martin and Banfield, Edward C.: *Politics, Planning and the Public Interest.* Glencoe, Illinois: The Free Press, 1955.

Morris, Robert and Binstock, Robert H.: *Feasible Planning for Social Change.* New York: Columbia University Press, 1966.

National Association of Social Workers: *Community Development and Social Work Practice.* Report of Workshop on Community Development in the United States Held at Brandeis University, April 8-12, 1962. New York: National Association of Social Workers, 1962.

National Association of Social Workers: *Encyclopedia of Social Work.* Edited by Harry Lurie. New York: National Association of Social Workers, 1965.

National Association of Social Workers: Report of the Preconference Workshop of the International Conference of Social Work. Held at Brandeis University, April 19-22, 1964, on "Social Work's Contribution to Social Planning, Progress, Problems, and Issues." New York: National Association of Social Workers, 1964.

Nelson, Lowry, Ramsey, Charles E., and Verner, Coalie: *Community Structure and Change.* New York: Macmillan, 1962.

Ross, Murray G.: *Community Organization, Theory, Principles and Practice,* 2nd ed. New York: Harper & Row, 1967.

THEORIES AND CONCEPTS OF SOCIAL PLANNING AND PLANNED CHANGE

American Institute of Planners: *Proceedings of the American Institute of Planners Conference,* Cambridge, Mass., 1960, vol. 43.

American Institute of Planners: *Proceedings of the American Institute of Planners Conference,* Cambridge, Mass., 1965, vol. 48.

Beal, George M.: Social Action: Instigated Social Change in Large Social System. In Copp, James H. (Ed.): *Our Changing Rural Society.* Ames: Iowa State University Press, 1964.

Bennis, Warren G., Benne, Kenneth D., and Chin, Robert (Eds.): *The Planning of Change.* New York: Holt, Rinehart and Winston, 1961.

Burke, Edmund M.: The search for authority in planning. *Social Service Review*, 41:250-260, September, 1967.

Council on Social Work Education: *Proceedings of 8th Annual Program Meeting*. New York, N.Y., 1960.

Dahl, Robert A. and Lindblom, Charles E.: Some social processes for rational calculation. In *Politics, Economics and Welfare*. New York: Harper & Bros., 1953.

David, Paul T.: Analytical approaches to the study of change. *Public Administration Review*, September, 1966, pp. 160-168.

Duhl, Leonard J.: Planning and predicting: Or what to do when you don't know the names of the variables. *Daedalus*, Summer, 1967, 779-788.

Foote, Nelson N. and Cottrell, Leonard S., Jr.: The Planning Process. In *Identity and Interpersonal Competence*. Chicago: University of Chicago Press, 1955.

Frieden, Bernard J. and Morris, Robert (Eds.): *Urban Planning and Social Policy*. New York: Basic Books, 1968.

Goodenough, Ward Hunt: *Cooperation in Change*. New York: Russell Sage Foundation, 1963.

Horowitz, Irving: The search for a development ideal: Alternative models and their implications. *The Sociological Quarterly*, 8: 427-438, Fall, 1967.

Jones, Garth N.: Strategies and tactics of planned organizational change: Case examples in the modernization process of traditional societies. *Human Organization*, 24 (Fall, 1965), 192-200.

Kahn, Alfred J. *Studies in Social Policy and Planning*. New York: Russell Sage Foundation, 1969.

Kahn, Alfred J.: *Theory and Practice of Social Planning*. New York: Russell Sage Foundation, 1969.

McLeish, John: *The Theory of Social Change: Four Views Considered*. New York: Schocken Books, 1968.

Millett, John D.: Planning. In *Management in the Public Service*. New York: McGraw-Hill, 1954.

Morris, Robert (Ed.): *Centrally Planned Change: Prospects and Concepts*. Report of a Workshop Held at Themis House, Weston, Mass., September, 1963. New York: National Association of Social Workers, 1964.

Morris, Robert: Social Planning. In Maas, Henry S. (Ed.): *Five Fields of Social Service*. New York: National Association of Social Workers, 1966.

Murphy, Campbell G.: *Community Organization Practice.* Boston: Houghton Mifflin, 1954.

Perloff, Harvey S.: New direction in social planning. *Journal of the American Institute of Planners, 31*:397-404, November, 1965.

Rothman, Jack: An analysis of goals and roles in community organization practice. *Social Work, 9*:24-31, April, 1964.

Simon, Herbert A., Smithburg, Donald W., and Thompson, Victor A.: The Strategy of Planning. *Public Administration.* New York: Knopf, 1950.

Sower, Christopher, *et al.*: *Community Involvement.* Glencoe, Illinois: The Free Press, 1957.

Thernstrom, Stephan: *Poverty, Planning and Politics in the New Boston.* New York: Basic Books, 1969.

Warren, Roland L.: *The Community in America.* Chicago: Rand McNally, 1963.

Warren, Roland L. (Ed.): *Perspectives on the American Community: A Book of Readings.* Chicago: Rand McNally, 1966.

Warren, Roland L. and Hyman, Herbert H.: Purposive community change in consensus and dissensus situations. *Community Mental Health Journal, 2*:293-300, Winter, 1966.

Wissman, Harold H.: *Community Development in the Mobilization for Youth Experience.* New York: Association Press, 1969.

Wood, Elizabeth: *Social Planning: A Primer for Urbanists.* Brooklyn N.Y.: Pratt Institute, 1965.

Zweig, Franklin M., and Morris, Robert: The social planning design guide: Process and proposal. *Social Work, 11*:13-21, April, 1966.

APPROACHES, METHODS, STRATEGIES, AND TACTICS FOR COMMUNITY ACTION

Ackoff, Russell L.: Towards a behavioral theory of communication. *Management Science, 4*:218-234, 1957.

Alinsky, Saul D.: *Reveille for Radicals.* Chicago: University of Chicago Press, 1946.

Barnlund, Dean C. (Comp.): *Interpersonal Communication.* Boston: Houghton Mifflin, 1968.

Brager, George: Advocacy and political behavior. *Social Work, 13*: 5-15, April, 1968.

Brager, George: Institutional Change: Perimeters of the Possible. *Social Work, 12*:59-69, January, 1967.

Brager, George and Jorrin, Valerie: Bargaining: A method in community change. *Social Work, 14*:73-83, October, 1969.

Cohen, Wilbur J.: What every social worker should know about political action. *Social Work, 11*:3-11, July, 1966.

Coughlin, Bernard: Community planning: A challenge to social work. *Social Work, 6*:37-42, October, 1961.

Cross, John G.: *The Economics of Bargaining.* New York: Basic Books, 1969.

Davidoff, Paul: Advocacy and pluralism in planning. *Journal of the American Institute of Planners, 31*:331-338, November, 1965.

Davidoff, Paul, Davidoff, Linda, and Gold, Neil Newton. Suburban action: Advocate planning for an open society. *Journal of the American Institute of Planners, 36*:12-21, January, 1970.

Davis, Floyd James: *Social Problems: Enduring Major Issues and Social Change.* New York: Free Press, 1970.

Dubey, Sumati N.: Community action programs and citizen participation: Issues and confusions. *Social Work, 15*:76-84, January, 1970.

Gilbert, Neil: *Clients or Constituents, Community Action in the War on Poverty.* San Francisco: Jossey-Bass, 1970.

Goetschius, George W.: *Working with Community Groups: Using Community Development as a Method of Social Work.* New York: Humanities Press, 1969.

Hillman, Arthur: *Community Organization and Planning.* New York: Macmillan, 1950.

Huenefeld, John: *The Community Activists Handbook.* Boston: Beacon Press, 1970.

Jaques, Elliott: Social Therapy: Technocracy or Collaboration? In Bennis, Warren G., Benne, Kenneth D., and Chin, Robert (Eds.): *The Planning of Change.* New York: Holt, Rinehart and Winston, 1961.

Kahn, Alfred: *Studies in Social Policy and Planning.* New York: Russell Sage Foundation, 1969.

Kramer, Ralph M.: *Participation of the Poor.* Englewood Cliffs, N.J.: Prentice-Hall, 1969.

Mott, Basil J. F.: The politics of health planning: II. The myth of planning without politics. *American Journal of Public Health, 59*: 797-803, May, 1969.

Moynihan, Daniel Patrick: *Maximum Feasible Misunderstanding.* New York: Free Press, 1969.

National Committee on Employment of Youth: *Source Book for Neighborhood Aids in Community Action Programs.* Prepared by Curriculum Development Project. Springfield, Virginia: Clearing house for Federal Scientific and Technical Information, 1967.

National Conference on Social Welfare: *Planning Social Services for Urban Needs.* Selected Papers, 84th Annual Forum of the National Conference on Social Welfare. Sieder, Violet M.: The Tasks of the Community Organization Worker. New York: Published for the National Conference on Social Welfare by Columbia University Press, 1957.

National Conference on Social Welfare: *Social Work Practice.* Selected Papers, 89th Annual Forum of the National Conference on Social Welfare. Rein, Martin and Morris, Robert: Goals, Structures, and Strategies for Community Change. New York: Published for the National Conference on Social Welfare by Columbia University Press, 1962.

Piven, Frances: Participation of residents in neighborhood community action programs. *Social Work, 11*:73-80, January, 1966.

Rein, Martin, and Riessman, Frank: A strategy for anti-poverty community action programs. *Social Work, 11*:3-12, April, 1966.

Ross, Murray G.: *Case Histories in Community Organization.* New York: Harper & Bros., 1958.

Sanders, Irwin T.: Professional Roles in Planned Change. In Morris, Robert (Ed.): *Centrally Planned Change: Prospects and Concepts.* New York: National Association of Social Workers, 1964.

Schelling, Thomas C.: *The Strategy of Conflict.* Cambridge, Mass.: Harvard University Press, 1960.

Schoonmaker, Alan N.: *What to Emphasize in Motivating People: Psychological Principles and Action Rules Can Aid Voluntary Organizations.* Reprinted from the Public Relations Journal, 1968.

Sherrard, Thomas D. (Ed.): *Social Welfare and Urban Problems.* New York: Published for the National Conference on Social Welfare (Columbus, Ohio) by Columbia University Press, 1968.

Simon, Herbert A., Smithburg, Donald W., and Thompson, Victor A.: The tactics of execution: Reducing the costs of change *and* The tactics of execution: Securing compliance. In *Public Administration.* New York: Alfred A. Knopf, 1950.

Specht, Harry: Disruptive tactics. *Social Work, 14*:5-15, April, 1969.

Spiegel, Hans B. C. (Ed.): *Citizen Participation in Urban Development.* Washington, D.C.: Center for Community Affairs, National Training Laboratories, Institute for Applied Behavioral Science, 1968.

Turner, John B. (Ed.): *Neighborhood Organization for Community Action.* New York: National Association of Social Workers, 1968.

United States Department of Health, Education, and Welfare, Administration on Aging: *To Tell the Story: A Public Information Guide for Project Directors.* Washington, D.C.: Government Printing Office, 1968.

Walton, Richard E.: Two strategies of social change and their dilemmas. *Journal of Applied Behavioral Science, 1*:167-179, April-May-June, 1965.

Warren, Roland L.: *Types of Purposive Social Change at the Community Level.* Brandeis University Papers in Social Welfare No. 11. Brandeis University, 1965.

Wilson, James Q.: Politics and planning: Citizen participation in urban renewal. *Journal of the American Institute of Planners, 29*:242-249, November, 1963.

Zurcher, Louis A. and Key, William H.: The overlap model: A comparison of strategies for social change. *Sociological Quarterly, 9*: 85-96, Winter, 1968.

STRUCTURAL OR ADMINISTRATIVE CONCERNS OF PLANNING

Beal, George M. *et al.*: *Social Action and Interaction in Program Planning.* Ames: Iowa State University Press, 1966.

Bennis, Warren G.: Theory and method in applying behavioral science to planned organizational change. *Journal of Applied Behavioral Science, 1*:337-360, October, November, December, 1966.

Bower, Joseph L.: Descriptive decision theory from the "administrative" viewpoint. In Bauer, Raymond A. and Gergin, Kenneth J. (Eds.): *The Study of Policy Formation.* New York: Free Press, 1968.

Carroll, Michael A.: *An Exploration of the Relationship between Urban Planning and Human Behavior: Toward the Identification of Professional Responsibilities.* Bloomington: Indiana University Press, 1968.

Golembiewski, Robert: Specialist or generalist: Structure as a crucial factor. *Public Administration Review, 25*:135-141, 1966.

Hatrey, Harry P. and Cotten, Joan J.: *Program Planning for State, County, City.* State-Local Finances Project. Washington, D.C.: George Washington University Press, 1967.

Kaplan, Howard B.: *Implementation of Program Change in Community Agencies: Studies of Organization Innovation.* Houston, Texas: Community Council, 1966.

Lippitt, R. J.: *Training in Community Relations.* New York: Harper & Bros., 1949.

Manser, Gordon: A critical look at community planning. *Social Work,* 5:35-41, April, 1960.

Morris, Robert and Randall, Ollie A.: Planning and organization of community services for the elderly. *Social Work, 10*:96-102, January, 1965.

National Conference on Social Welfare: *Social Work Practice.* Selected Papers, 90th Annual Forum of the National Conference on Social Welfare. Morris, Robert and Rein, Martin: Emerging Patterns in Community Planning. New York: Published for the National Conference on Social Welfare by Columbia University Press, 1963.

National Conference on Social Welfare: *The Social Welfare Forum 1965.* Schorr, Alvin L.: The Future Structure of Community Services. New York: Published for the National Conference on Social Welfare by Columbia University Press, 1965.

Poston, Richard W.: *Experiment in North Carolina.* Report on the Community Services Demonstration Program of the North Carolina State Department of Public Welfare. Chapel Hill, N.C.: University of North Carolina, School of Social Work, 1967.

Rein, Martin: Organization for social change. *Social Work, 9*:32-41, 1964.

Zald, Mayer N.: Organizations as politics: An analysis of community organization agencies. *Social Work, 11*:56-65, October, 1966.

STUDY OF THE COMMUNITY

Auerbach, Arnold: Aspirations of power people and agency goals. *Social Work, 6*:66-73, January, 1961.

Banfield, Edward C.: *Political Influence.* New York: Free Press of Glencoe, 1961.

Bernard, Jessie S.: *American Community Behavior,* rev. ed. New York: Holt, Rinehart and Winston, 1962.

Bernard, Jessie S.: Social-psychological aspects of community study: Some areas comparatively neglected by American sociologists. *British Journal of Sociology, II*:12-30, March, 1951.

Clark, Terry M.: Power and community structure: Who governs, where, and when? *The Sociological Quarterly,* 8:291-316, Summer, 1967.

Clark, Terry M.: *Community Structure and Decision Making.* San Francisco: Chandler Publishing, 1968.

Form, William H. and Sauer, Warren L.: *Community Influentials in a Middle-Sized City: A Case Study,* East Lansing: Michigan State

University, The Institute for Community Development and Services, 1960.

Fox, Douglas M.: The identification of community leaders by the reputational and decisional methods—Three case studies and an empirical analysis of the literature. *Sociology and Social Research,* 54:94-102, October, 1969.

Freeman, Linton C.: *Patterns of Social Community Leadership.* Indianapolis: Bobbs-Merrill, 1968.

Freeman, Linton C. *et al.:* Locating leaders in local communities: A comparison of some alternative approaches. *American Sociological Review,* 28:791-798, October, 1963.

Gamberg, Herbert: The professional and policy choices in middle-sized cities. *Journal of the American Institute of Planners, 32:* 174-177, May, 1966.

Gamson, William A.: Reputation and resources in community politics. *American Journal of Sociology,* 72:121-131, September, 1966.

Gore, William J. and Hodapp, Leroy C. (Eds.): *Change in the Small Community,* New York: Friendship Press, 1967.

Green, James W. and Mayo, Selz C.: A framework for research in the actions of community groups. *Social Forces, 31:*320-326, May, 1953.

Hunter, Floyd: *Community Power Structure: A Study of Decision Makers.* Chapel Hill: University of North Carolina Press, 1953.

Hunter, Floyd: Community Power Structure and Social Welfare: In Stein, Herman D. and Cloward, Richard A. (Eds.): *Social Perspectives on Behavior.* New York: Free Press of Glencoe, 1958.

Institute of Community and Area Development and University of Georgia, *Community Social Analysis Series.* Atlanta: University of Georgia, Institute of Community and Area Development, Nos. 1-5, 1965-1967.

Kaufman, Harold F.: Toward an Interactional Conception of Community. In Warren, Roland (Ed.): *Perspectives on the American Community.* Chicago: Rand-McNally, 1966.

Mann, Lawrence D.: Studies in community decision making. *Journal of the American Institute of Planners, 30:*58-65, February, 1964.

Morris, Robert: Basic factors in planning for the coordination of health services. *American Journal of Public Health, 53:*248-259, February, 1963.

Morris, Robert: Basic factors in planning for the coordination of health services. *American Journal of Public Health, 53:*462-472, March, 1963.

Nelson, Lowry, Ramsey, Charles E., and Verner, Coalie: *Community Structure and Change*. New York: Macmillan, 1960.

Odegard, Peter H.: *Political Power and Social Change*. New Brunswick, N.J.: Rutgers University Press, 1966.

Polsby, Nelson W.: Three problems in the analysis of community power. *American Sociological Review, 24:*796-803, December, 1959.

Polsby, Nelson W.: The sociology of community power: A reassessment. *Social Forces, 37:*232-236, 1959.

Presthus, Robert: *Men at the Top: A Study in Community Power*. New York: Oxford University Press, 1964.

Rabinovitz, Francine F.: The real world of municipal politics. *City Politics and Planning*. New York: Atherton Press, 1969.

Raven, B. and French, J.: The Bases of Social Power. In Cartwright, Dorwin and Zander, Alvin (Eds.): *Group Dynamics*. Evanston, Ill.: Row and Peterson, 1960.

Sollie, Carlton R.: A comparison of reputational techniques for identifying community leaders. *Rural Sociology, 31:*301-309, September, 1966.

Spenald, William: Power in local communities. *Social Problems, 12:* 335-356, Winter, 1965.

Taber, Merlin, Itzin, Frank, and Turner, William: *A Comprehensive Analysis of Health and Welfare Services for Older Persons in One Community*. Iowa City: Institute of Gerontology, State University of Iowa, 1963.

Wachtel, Dawn Day: Structures of community and strategies for organization. *Social Work, 13:*85-91, January, 1968.

Warren, Roland: *Studying Your Community*. New York: Russell Sage Foundation, 1955.

White, James E.: Theory and method for research in community leadership. *American Sociological Review, 15:*50-60, 1950.

Young, Pauline V.: *Scientific Social Surveys and Research*, 4th ed. Englewood Cliffs, N.J.: Prentice-Hall, 1966.

DECISION-MAKING

Alexis, Marcus and Wilson, Charles Z.: *Organizational Decision Making*. Englewood Cliffs, N.J.: Prentice-Hall, Inc., 1967.

Becker, Gordon M. and McClintock, Charles G.: Value: Behavioral decision theory. *Annual Review of Psychology, 18:*239-286, 1967.

Braybrooke, David and Lindblom, Charles E.: *A Strategy of Decision: Policy Evaluation as a Social Process*. New York: Free Press, 1963.

Cleveland, Richard F.: The Margin of Malleability. In Reed, Ella W.: *Social Welfare Administration*. New York: Columbia University Press, 1961.

Community Fund of Chicago and Welfare Council of Metropolitan Chicago. *Community Fund of Chicago, Inc., Part 1: Priorities, Recommended Criteria for Agency Performance and Priorities of Community Fund Support of Agency Services*. Chicago: Fund of Chicago and the Welfare Council of Metropolitan Chicago, 1967.

Edwards, Ward and Tversky, Amos: *Decision Making*. Penguin Books. Baltimore: Harmondsworth, 1967.

Etzioni, Amitai: Mixed-scanning: A "third" approach to decision-making. *Public Administration Review*, 27:385-392.

Gore, William J.: *Administrative Decision-Making: An Heuristic Model*. New York: John Wiley & Sons, 1964.

Hill, Morris: A goals-achievement matrix for evaluating alternative plans. *Journal of the American Institute of Planners*, XXIV:19-29, 1968.

Kramer, Ralph and Denton, Clare: Organization of a community action program: A comparative case study. *Social Work, 12*:68-80, October, 1967.

Lindblom, Charles E.: *The Intelligence of Democracy: Decision Making Through Mutual Adjustment*. New York: Free Press, 1965.

Miller, Paul A.: The process of decision-making within the context of community organization. *Rural Sociology*, XVII:153-161, June, 1952.

Perloff, Harvey S.: Planning concepts and regional research. *Social Forces, 32*:173-177, December, 1953.

Rein, Martin: Social science and the elimination of poverty. *Journal of the American Institute of Planners*, 33:146-163, May, 1967.

Schuetz, Alfred: Choosing among projects of action. *Philosophy and Phenomenological Research*, XII:161-184, December, 1951.

Simon, Herbert A.: *Administrative Behavior*. New York: Macmillan, 1955.

Simon, Herbert A.: *Models of Man*. New York: Wiley, 1957.

Taylor, Donald W.: Decision-Making and Problem Solving. In March, James C. (Ed.): *Handbook of Organizations*. Chicago: Rand McNally, 1965.

Thompson, James D. and Tuden, Arthur: Strategies, structures, and processes of organizational decision. *Comparative Studies in Administration*. Edited by the Staff of the Administrative Science Center. Pittsburgh: University of Pittsburgh Press, 1959.

United Community Funds and Councils of America: *Priorities in Community Services.* New York: United Community Funds and Councils of America, Bulletin 214, 1960.

Young, Robert C.: Goals and goal setting. *Journal of the American Institute of Planners,* 32:76-85, March, 1966.

FEEDBACK, EVALUATION, AND CORRECTION

Goldman, Thomas A.: Cost Effectiveness Analysis. In *New Approaches in Decision-Making.* New York: Frederick A. Praeger, 1967.

Hayes, Samuel P., Jr.: *Evaluating Development Projects: A Manual for the Use of Field Workers,* 2nd ed. New York: UNESCO Publications Center, 1966.

Holland, John B., Tiedke, Kenneth E., and Miller, Paul A.: A theoretical model for health action. *Rural Sociology, XXII:*149-155, June, 1957.

International Conference of Social Work: *Social Progress Through Social Planning—The Role of Social Work.* Report of the U.S. Committee to the XIIth International Conference of Social Work, Athens, Greece, September, 1964. Dumpson, James R.: Planning by Social Agencies. New York: International Conference of Social Work, 1965.

Merci, Wayne R.: Social action and research perspective. *Journal of Human Relations, XIV:*294-305, Second Quarter, 1966.

Miller, George A., Galanter, Eugene, and Priban, Karl H.: Plans and the Structure of Behavior. In Buckley, Walter (Ed.): *Modern Systems Research for the Behavioral Scientist.* Chicago: Aldine, 1968.

Slack, Charles W.: Feedback theory and the reflex arc concept. In Buckley, Walter (Ed.): *Modern Systems Research for the Behavioral Scientist.* Chicago: Aldine, 1968.

United States Department of Health, Education, and Welfare. *Evaluation in Mental Health.* Washington, D.C.: Government Printing Office, 1955.

Wilson, A. G.: Forecasting "Planning." *Urban Studies, VI:*347-367,

NAME INDEX

205

SUBJECT INDEX

A

Accountability, 21-25, 69-70
Action,
  guidelines for, 58-70, 118-22
    external, 58-62, 118-20
      control of bargaining assets, 58, 118
      control input of information, 58-59, 118
      dissemination of information, 61-62, 119
      recipients of information, 61, 119
      style of communication, 60-61, 119
      tactics for action, 62-66, 119-21
      timing, 60, 119
      use of opportunistic situations, 59-60, 119
      see also Tactics
    internal, 67-70, 120-22
      be accountable, 21, 69-70, 121-22
      focus on payoffs and outcome, 20, 67, 120
      keep available and use information, 20-21, 68, 120-21
      make rational decisions, 21, 69, 121
      receive feedback, 21, 68-69, 121
      safeguard time, 20, 67-68, 120
  internal procedures for, 71-106
    feedback and correction, 68-69, 71-95, 120-24
    Forecast Sheets, 72-73, 77-78, 122-23
    Journal Sheets, 74, 79-83, 123
    Review and Appraisal Sheets, 75, 87-90, 123-24
    Time Tally Sheets, 76, 91-94, 124

    organizing information, 95-106
      on Action Worksheets, 95-96
      on resource files, 96-106
      see also Files
Action on Aging, see Trial effort
Action File, 105-06, 110, 124
  change aids category in, 105-06
  definition of, 187
  written action materials in, 105, 124
Action period, 72, 78
Action Worksheets, 48-52, 95-96, 113-15
  as active reference sources, 95-96
  care in external use of, 104
  definition of, 48-49, 95, 187
  example of, 144-65
  filing of, 104-05
  outline for, 49-52, 95, 113-15
    change aids, 50-52, 114-15
    changes possible, 52, 115
    nature and extent of problem, 49-50, 114
    potential lines of activity, 52, 115
    problem situation in life arena, 49, 113
    services dealing with problem, 50, 114
    see also Change aids
  purposes of, 49
  start when, 113
Activity, see Line of activity
Advise
  definition of, 187
  tactic of, 66, 121
Advocate, 5, 24
Agency, see Community Agency and Organization File
Aids, see Change Aids
Ameliorate conflict
  definition of, 187
  tactic of, 65-66, 121
Appraisal, see Review and Appraisal Sheets

208